GUIDE TO Colorado Wildflowers

Plains and Foothills

Photography, watercolors
and text by G. K. Guennel

I respectfully dedicate this book to the memory of my inspiring teachers at Butler University: John E. Potzger and Ray C. Friesner.

"Oh my God! That's the most beautiful thing I've ever seen." — **Hilde E. Guennel,** my loving and caring wife of half a century, when we found the exquisite calypso orchid, the aptly named Fairy Slipper.

Acknowledgments

I owe special thanks to Janet L. Wingate, Ph.D., and Loraine Yeatts of the Kathryn Kalbach Herbarium at the Denver Botanic Gardens who helped me with identifications and, hopefully, kept me from making a fool of myself. Any errors, whatever their nature, are mine and mine alone.

International Standard Book Number:
1-56579-118-5

Library of Congress Catalog Number:
95-60672

Copyright:
G. K. Guennel, 1995. All Rights Reserved

Managing Editor:
Suzanne Venino, Westcliffe Publishers

Assistant Editors:
Dougald MacDonald
Sallie M. Greenwood

Design:
Rebecca Finkel, F + P Graphic Design

Published by
Westcliffe Publishers, Inc.
2650 South Zuni Street
Englewood, Colorado 80110

Manufactured in China by
Palace Press International

Introduction

During some thirty years of botanizing in Colorado, I used more than fifty books to identify plants. Apparently I was not alone. Friends and fellow hobbyists frequently expressed frustration in identifying plants, convincing me of the need for a comprehensive flower guide aimed at the layperson. The overwhelming need, expressed time and again, was for pictures, pictures, pictures.

The easiest way to identify an unknown plant is to compare it to a picture; the average person doesn't want or need botanical jargon. So when I started cataloging plants, I stressed color and pictures—painting watercolors and taking color photographs. The cliché "a picture is worth a thousand words" took on new meaning and real importance. It became a truism, and I became a true believer.

Although trained as a botanist, I consider my Colorado botanizing a hobby, for I earned my living dealing with fossil plants—primarily pollen and spores —not living ones. I relied heavily upon H. D. Harrington's *Manual of Plants of Colorado* (1964) and William A. Weber's two books, *Colorado Flora, Western Slope* (1987) and *Colorado Flora, Eastern Slope* (1990). Supplementing these "bibles" with many other sources, I was able to identify the plants I had collected and photographed over the years. The descriptive material that I extracted from these publications, I integrated with my own observations to compile the brief descriptions that accompany the watercolors and photographs.

Which species to include and how many was indeed a challenging question. Harrington lists 3,078 flowering plants and conifers, i.e., angiosperms and gymnosperms, respectively—far too many for a field guide with a description and two illustrations per species. I decided upon approximately 600 species that I consider to be fairly representative of what the average person might find.

The majority of plant species treated in these two volumes are wildflowers —flowering plants that grow in the wild. The term "wildflower" may be some-what misleading, however, for this guide covers much more. While the average person may not recognize the reproductive structures of grasses and sedges as flowers, they are, nevertheless, flowers by definition, as are the reproductive organs of willow and cottonwood trees. I am, however, overstepping the boundaries of the term "flowers" when I include coniferous trees, such as pines and spruces. But if cottonwoods are covered here, why not blue spruces or bristlecone pines? They grow in the same places you find columbines and paintbrushes, and it would be hard not to notice them and be curious.

These two volumes are the culmination of some thirty years of study and research. With the pictures and text presented here, it is my hope that you will find enjoyment and satisfaction, as I have over the years, in discovering and identifying Colorado's wildflowers.

How to Use This Guide

An understanding of the overall organization of this guide will help you in identifying the flora of Colorado. First, it was necessary to divide the work into two volumes. Within each volume, I grouped plants by color, and then I split off trees/shrubs from herbs. Lastly, I listed the plants alphabetically by family, and within each family, alphabetically by common name. The explanations below elaborate more fully on this organization.

VOLUME 1 and VOLUME 2

Because of the sheer number and diversity of plants that grow in Colorado, this guide has been divided into two volumes. Volume 1 covers species you will most likely find in the plains and foothills—the life zones found between 3,500 and 8,000 feet in elevation. Volume 2 covers plants you will find in the mountains, above 8,000 feet, in the montane, subalpine, and alpine life zones. For more about Colorado's life zones, read the introductory text starting on page 8.

COLOR

Within each volume, plants have been grouped by color for easy identification. A color bar on each page indicates whether you are in the green, white, yellow, red, blue, or purple section. Because color is the most obvious and striking characteristic of flowers, it makes sense to group them this way. There are, however, some drawbacks. What may appear red to me, may look orange to you. Or, a particular flower may be multi-colored, with white, purple, and red petals, and thus could be placed in three separate color sections. And what about species that produce individuals of different colors? Rosy paintbrush, for instance, can have pink, magenta, red, lavender, or purple bracts.

In order to keep these two books to a convenient size, it was necessary to select one color designation for each species. Keep in mind, however, that more than one color possibility may exist and that you may need to look for a given flower under more than one color. For example, if a flower is pink to lavender, look in this guide under red and purple.

The green section needs some explanation, since it is a catchall grouping for species that lack the more typical, showy colors associated with flowers. The flowering organs of grasses and sedges, as well as trees such as cottonwoods and willows, are basically green. Conifer trees—pines, spruces, firs, and junipers—have no flowers, yet their reproductive structures are primarily green or brown; these are included in the green section.

TREES/SHRUBS or HERBS

Most people can recognize a tree or a shrub by their large size and hard, woody stems and branches. Herbs, on the other hand, are neither woody nor large, but fleshy and generally small. I combined trees and shrubs into a single category (because they are relatively few in number) and arranged each color section so that the trees and shrubs appear first, followed by herbs. So if you were to come across a shrub with red flowers, you would turn to the red tabbed pages and look at the beginning of that section under the TREES/SHRUBS heading. Conversely, if you came across a plant with red flowers that was obviously not a tree or a shrub, you would look in the red section under the HERBS heading.

Keep in mind, however, that there are trees and shrubs that are small in stature, such as the dwarfed willows and birches of the alpine zone. And there are herbs that reach ten feet in height. Nevertheless, I believe that creating one category for large, woody plants and another category for small, fleshy ones is a useful step in helping you locate a species in question.

PLANT FAMILIES

Species within the trees/shrubs heading are listed alphabetically by family, as are species under the herbs heading. A family represents a natural grouping of plants that are related through similar characteristics. Once you've chosen a color category and determined if an unknown flower is an herb, a tree, or a shrub, knowing the general family characteristics can prove helpful in deciding where to look in this guide.

If, for example, you can recognize a composite flower head, which is characteristic of the Aster family (a large family that includes daisies, sunflowers, goldenrods, and sages), you can limit your search to that family. Or, if you can identify a plant as a grass, or recognize the unique structure of a pea flower, then you can go directly to the alphabetical listings of those families. Thus the number of pages you need to flip through to compare a unknown flower to those in the book can be limited to one family at a time.

I believe I can guide you to a number of families simply by pointing out the more obvious characteristics of the larger families and the peculiarities of some of the others. Listed below are easily recognized families:

Aster family: composite flower heads *
Borage family: hairy appearance and tubular flowers
Cactus family: fleshy, leafless and spiny; with showy flowers
Celery family: flowers in umbels and compound, deeply dissected leaves
Evening Primrose family: long corolla tube, four petals, and eight stamens
Figwort family: two-sided flowers and opposite leaves
Grass family: green herbs with inconspicuous flowers and narrow leaves *

Knotweed family: hard, triangular fruit and knotlike nodes with papery sheaths
Mint family: square stems and aromatic, two-lipped flowers
Mustard family: four petals that form a cross
Pea family: beanlike seed pods; flowers with banner, keel, and two wings *
Rose family: five petals in radial symmetry and leaves in stipules
Sedge family: resembles grasses but have sharp, triangular stems
Willow family: all trees and shrubs, with catkins

See glossary for illustrations of these flower types.

SPECIES DESCRIPTIONS

Each page in this guide is devoted to a single plant species. The species description consists of three components:

1. Common, Scientific, and Family Name
2. Plant Description
3. Habitat, Life Zones, and Flowering Time

Common, Scientific, and Family Name

Each wildflower in this guide is listed by its common name, which appears at the top of the page in large, bold letters. It is in English and is the name most often used in the literature. It is not unusual for a flower to be known by more than one common name. Alpine Fireweed, for instance, is also known as Low Fireweed, Broadleaved Fireweed, Broadleaved Willowherb, Dwarf Fireweed, Red Willowherb, and River Beauty. Alternate common names are listed in parentheses.

Below the common name is the plant's scientific name. Scientific names, which are in Latin and are italicized, are based on an internationally accepted system of nomenclature that identifies a plant species anywhere in the world. While common names may be more descriptive, understandable, whimsical, and pronounceable, they are not reliable for scientific comparisons; for the same common name may also be applied to a number of different plants. I have followed William A. Weber's nomenclature throughout this guide. After all, he is the guru of Colorado plant taxonomy.

Most scientific names are binomials, that is, made up of two names. The first name refers to the genus (capitalized) and the second refers to the species (lowercased). For example, *Helianthus* (genus: sunflower) is combined with *pumilus* (species: dwarf) to form the scientific name *Helianthus pumilus.* Some scientific names are trinomials, should a species be split into subspecies.

Scientific names undergo changes from time to time. For example, a well-established name may have to be abandoned if it is proven that the species in question was described earlier under a different name, in which case, the older name has priority. Such name changes are governed by strict rules and documentation requirements. When a plant has had a history of previous scientific names, I have included them in parentheses below the currently accepted scientific name.

Following the common and scientific names is the name of the plant family, with its Latin equivalent in parentheses.

Plant Description

Next is an overall description of the plant, its general appearance, size, distinguishing characteristics, flowers, and leaves. This information has been extracted from the literature and was augmented by my own observations. I have tried to avoid botanical jargon and technical terminology wherever possible. When I could not avoid doing so, I have either explained the term within its context, included it in the glossary, or both.

Measurements are given in inches or feet, rather than in metric equivalents, because I believe the average person in the United States is not yet familiar with the metric system. Also, I have listed maximum dimensions—providing the upper limit of sizes instead of an average or an overall range.

Habitat, Life Zones, and Flowering Time

The last three items tell you where and when to look for the plant. Habitat is given first, listing the various environments in which the plant is found — whether it grows on rocky tundra slopes, for instance, or is more likely to be found along moist stream banks and lake shores. Again, I have added my own observations to information reported in the literature.

The range of life zones is listed next. Most wildflowers grow in more than one life zone. The common dandelion, for example, occurs in all five life zones: plains, foothills, montane, subalpine, and alpine.

Flowering time specifies the months when you will most likely find the flower in bloom. I have found the literature inadequate in citing such data, and in many instances I had to rely on my own observations. Keep in mind that flowering times are affected by elevation; plants growing at higher elevations will generally bloom later than the same species growing at lower elevations.

WATERCOLORS and PHOTOGRAPHS

Watercolors were drawn to scale but are printed in this book at approximately 75 to 80 percent of original size. Color photographs are not to scale; they show close-up details or the overall appearance of the plant.

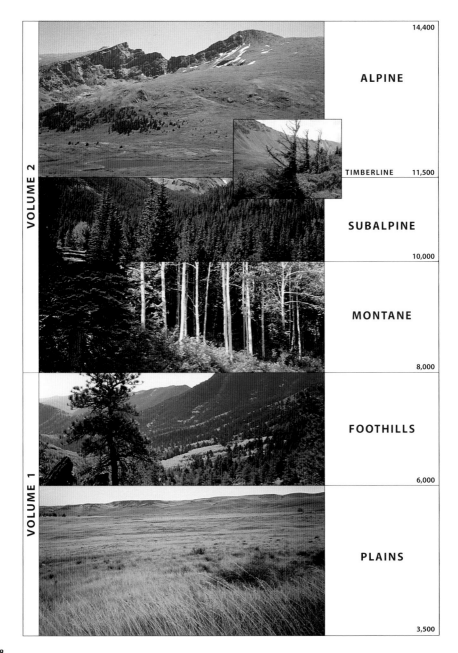

VOLUME 2

14,400

ALPINE

TIMBERLINE 11,500

SUBALPINE

10,000

MONTANE

8,000

VOLUME 1

FOOTHILLS

6,000

PLAINS

3,500

Colorado's Life Zones

Why a plant grows in a certain place is determined by many factors. Climate is the dominant influence; soil chemistry and biological factors are also important. In Colorado, topography and altitude are of particular significance, as there is an elevation of more than 11,000 vertical feet from the Great Plains to the summits of the Rocky Mountains.

Based on ecosystems and plant communities, and delineated by elevation, five distinct life zones have been defined in Colorado: the plains, foothills, montane, subalpine, and alpine zones. They correspond to the Sonoran, Transitional, Canadian, Hudsonian, and Arctic zones of the North American systems, which is based on latitude. In this comparison, where every 1,000 feet in elevation equals 600 miles in distance on the ground, driving from the town of Holly, Colorado, (elevation 3,386 feet) to the top of Mount Elbert (the state's highest peak at 14,433 feet) is the equivalent of traveling from Mexico to the Arctic Circle.

PLAINS ZONE — 3,500 to 6,000 Feet

Covering the eastern third of the state, the high plains of Colorado are primarily mixed-grass prairie, a grassland ecosystem. Where sandy hills or dunes interrupt the grassland, shrubs (sagebrush, rabbitbrush, snakeweed) take over, along with yucca and cacti. The trees of the plains (cottonwoods, willows, and boxelders) are restricted to streamsides and riverbanks. Although semi-arid, the plains are extremely rich in wildflowers. The Pawnee Buttes and Comanche Grasslands are especially noteworthy.

In the western part of the state, the equivalent of the plains life zone starts at about 4,500 feet on the Colorado Plateau. It is characterized by vast areas of sagebrush, shrubby desert plants, and sparse grasses. In spring and early summer, the slopes are aglow with bright wildflowers. Higher up pinyon and juniper grow in close association.

FOOTHILLS ZONE — 6,000 to 8,000 Feet

In western Colorado, the pinyon-juniper association extends into the foothills. In eastern Colorado this zone is characterized by shrubs, dominated by scrub oak, mountain mahogany, three-leaf sumac, and common juniper. (The juniper of the western pinyon-juniper association is actually a cedar of the genus *Sabina*, not *Juniperus*.) Ponderosa pines, Douglas firs, blue spruces, and scattered aspens form open woodlands. Foothills flowers are abundant and diverse; too often transplanted by gardeners, they are literally being loved to death.

MONTANE ZONE — 8,000 to 10,000 Feet

The open woods of the foothills become a tighter, more cohesive forest in the montane. The addition of lodgepole and limber pines to the ponderosa pine-Douglas fir-blue spruce association, plus large aspen groves, give the montane zone a distinct look. The montane forest supports a rich understory of grasses and wildflowers. Shrubs grow in clearings and along the forests' edge. At the upper elevations of this zone, you find white fir (south of Colorado Springs) and bristlecone pine (south of Berthoud Pass).

The montane harbors large open areas known as mountain parks. North Park, Middle Park, South Park, and the San Luis Valley are vast meadows of grasses and sedges dotted with wildflowers. To see bistort, shooting star, little red elephant, or wild iris in such great profusion is a breathtaking experience.

SUBALPINE ZONE — 10,000 to 11,500 Feet

Dense forests of Engelmann spruce and subalpine fir dominate the subalpine zone. These tall, stately giants—they can reach 100 feet in height—form a distinctive dark green cape that drapes the shoulders of the mountain peaks. This is the zone of the hunters' "black timber," and the area carved up by ski slopes. Because showers are frequent and snow is sheltered by the dense growth of trees, water is abundant and forms pools, bogs, and swamps. Undergrowth, however, is sparse and limited to the forest edges and clearings. Along rivulets and in meadows, you find luxurious carpets of wildflowers. The dark, somber forest hides wood nymphs and Jacob's ladders, bog orchids and fairy slippers.

TIMBERLINE — About 11,500 Feet

Timberline—or treeline—is the boundary between the subalpine and alpine zones. Above this line the forests give way to tundra and trees no longer grow. Timberline is generally considered at 11,500 feet, although it is higher in the south (12,000 feet on Pikes Peak) and lower in the north (about 11,000 in Rocky Mountain National Park). It may zigzag up and down a few hundred feet in any given area, creeping upward on protected southern exposures and scooting down on cooler, north-facing slopes.

Harsh, drying winds and cold temperatures twist bristlecone pine and Engelmann spruce into stunted versions of those found at lower elevations. These misshapen trees, known as krummholz—German for "crooked wood"—are obvious indicators that you are at timberline.

ALPINE ZONE — 11,500 to 14,400 Feet

The treeless, windswept landscape of the alpine zone, the uppermost life zone, is commonly called tundra. Unlike the Siberian tundra, permanently frozen lowlands covered with mosses and lichens, the alpine tundra of Colorado is a high-altitude environment defined by sedges and grasses. Both environments are harsh and inhospitable.

The soils of the alpine zone are thin and porous, retaining little moisture. The sun's rays are strong, the winds fierce and relentless. Plants here have adapted to this severe environment. They grow low to the ground and protect themselves from heat, cold, and desiccating wind with cuticle and hair. By growing rapidly and producing seeds early, alpine plants not only manage to survive, but to thrive.

The sedges and grasses form a tight sod that anchors and holds the soil in place. Where the sedge/grass carpet is interrupted, dwarf shrubs move in and low herbs establish their own cushions and turf mats. Most alpine plants bloom in late June and early July, turning the alpine wasteland into a kaleidoscope of color.

Sand Sage

(Sand Sagebrush, Silvery
 Wormwood, Three-Leaved
 Wormwood)

Oligosporus filifolius
(Artemisia filifolia)

Aster Family (Asteraceae)

Shrub, to 5' tall, with slender,
tannish stems and whitish, hairy
twigs. Grows in tight clumps.

Flower heads are small and many,
in narrow panicles, with only 3 ray
flowers and 6 disk flowers. Flowers
are often crippled by galls.

Leaves are divided into angular,
silvery, hairy, threadlike segments.

Grows in dry and sandy areas on
the eastern plains.

Life Zone: Plains

Flowering Time: July and August

Scrub Oak

(Gambel's Oak)

Quercus gambelii
(Q. confusa, Q. gunnisonii, Q. leptophylla,
Q. neomexicana, Q. undulata, Q. utahensis)

Beech Family (Fagaceae)

Small tree or shrub, to 20' tall, with reddish brown twigs and gray bark. Forms thickets by suckers.

Flowers are separated by sex. Male flowers are greenish, have long tassels, and form 1" long catkins; female flowers also are greenish but are tiny and clustered in leaf axils. Acorns are less than 1" long, with a basal cup.

Leaves are alternate, to 6" long, shiny, leathery, and deeply cut into rounded lobes.

Grows on dry slopes, along roads, and in open woods.

Life Zones: Plains to Montane

Flowering Time: April to June

13

Beaked Hazelnut

(Hazelnut, Filbert)

Corylus cornuta

Birch Family (Betulaceae)

Shrub, to 6' tall, with smooth bark and smooth, brownish twigs.

Male and female flowers are separate but on same plant. Male flowers are arranged in pendant catkins that overwinter; female flowers are clustered. The nut is ovoid, to ⅝" long, and constricted into a beak.

Leaves are ovate, to 4¾" long, with pointed tips and toothed margins.

Grows in thickets at the edges of woods, along creeks, and in forest clearings and ravines.

Life Zone: Foothills

Flowering Time: April and May

Paper Birch

(Canoe Birch, White Birch,
Western White Birch)

Betula papyrifera

Birch Family (Betulaceae)

Tree or shrub, to 80' tall, with open
crown, papery white bark with horizontal
fissures, and slender, reddish, sticky twigs.

Male and female flowers are
separate but on the same tree.
Male catkins are drooping, to
4" long; female catkins are
erect and less than 1⅜" long.

Leaves are ovate, to 4½" long,
thick, firm, yellowish beneath,
with toothed margins.

Found in cool, shady areas,
on north-facing slopes.

Life Zone: Foothills

Flowering Time: April and June

One-Seed Juniper

(Cherrystone Juniper)

Sabina monosperma
(Juniperus monosperma)

Cypress Family (Cupressaceae)

Tree or shrub, to 30' tall, with gray, shredded bark and stout, 4-sided, reddish brown branchlets.

Cones are segregated by sex on separate treees. Male cones are small and inconspicuous; female cones are berrylike, with bluish bloom and a single, 4-sided seed.

Leaves are ⅛" long and overlap like scales, with sharp tips and gland on back.

Grows in dry areas of southern Colorado, such as mesas, rocky slopes, and deserts.

Life Zones: Plains and Foothills

Flowering Time: June and July

Fourwing Saltbush

(Chico, Orache, Chamisco)

Atriplex canescens

Goosefoot Family
(Chenopodiaceae)

Shrub, to 3' tall, with white stem and slender, stiff branches.

Flowers are inconspicuous, in woolly, scaly clusters; bracts have 4 wings.

Leaves are alternate, grayish, to 1" long.

Common in sandy and alkaline areas.

Life Zones:
Plains and Foothills

Flowering Time:
July and August

Wild Grape

(Riverbank Grape, Fox Grape, Frost Grape)

Vitis riparia
(V. vulpina, V. longii)

Grape Family (Vitaceae)

Woody, climbing vine with peeling, grayish brown bark and bright green to reddish branchlets with tendrils.

Flowers are tiny, in elongate clusters. Petals drop off when stamens mature. Grapes are green to bluish black, to ⁷/₁₆" across.

Leaves are large (to 4" by 6") and cut into 3 lobes, tannish white underneath.

Grows along streams and rivers, in canyons and gulches, in thickets and the borders of woods, and along roads.

Life Zones: Plains and Foothills

Flowering Time: May to July

Mormon Tea

(Jointfir, Squaw Tea, Cowboy Tea,
  Clapweed, Ephedra)

Ephedra viridis

Jointfir Family (Ephedraceae)

Shrub, to 3' tall, stemless but much-branched, leafless, and scraggly.

Male and female cones are on separate plants. Male cones have pale green bracts and are less than ⅜" long; female cones reach ½" and have reddish, fleshy bracts.

Leaves are scalelike and whitish, to ⅛" long, and arise at nodes in pairs.

Grows in western Colorado in rocky or gravelly areas, such as rim rock, ledges, canyons, and ravines.

Life Zones: Plains to Montane

Flowering Time: May

Boxelder

(Ash-Leaved Maple)

Negundo aceroides
(Acer negundo)

Maple Family (Aceraceae)

Tree or shrub, to 60' tall, with dark gray bark and bluish, stout twigs.

Flowers are segregated by sex on separate trees. Male flowers are in large, drooping, pink catkins; female flowers are in greenish clusters. Fruit is paired, 1½" long, and winged.

Leaves are opposite and divided into 3 to 7 coarse-toothed, reddish-stalked leaflets.

Grows in moist places, such as canyons, gulches, streamsides, and riverbanks.

Life Zones: Plains and Foothills

Flowering Time: April and May

White Mulberry
Morus alba

Mulberry Family (Moraceae)

Tree or shrub, to 50' high, with milky sap, rounded crown, spreading branches, and slender, cream-colored, peeling twigs.

Flowers are small and segregated by sex on separate branches or even separate trees. Male flowers are in erect clusters; female flowers are in drooping clusters. Fruit is berrylike, whitish to pale red.

Leaves are coarse-toothed, to 4" long, smooth, and often 3-lobed.

Grows along fences and roads, and on abandoned land; Asian import that escaped cultivation.

Life Zones:
Plains and Foothills

Flowering Time:
April and May

Pinyon Pine

(Nut Pine, Colorado Pinyon)

Pinus edulis
(Caryopitys edulis)

Pine Family (Pinaceae)

Bushy tree, to 45' high, with scaly, gray to brown bark, and orange to gray twigs.

Male cones are small, clustered at branch tips, and red. Female cones are squat (to 2" long) with tan, woody scales. Seeds are brown and edible.

Needles are short (2" long), stiff, ascending or curved, mostly in pairs, light green, with pointed tips.

Common in southern and western Colorado on mesas, rocky slopes, and ridges.

Life Zones: Plains and Foothills

Pollinating Time: May

Cottonwood

(Plains Cottonwood)

Populus deltoides monilifera
(P. sargentii, P. occidentalis)

Willow Family (Salicaceae)

Tree, to 100' tall, massive, with thick, furrowed, gray bark and smooth, yellow, stout twigs.

Flowers are segregated by sex on separate trees. Male catkins are dense, thick, and less than 2½" long; female catkins are open clusters, to 8" long; both are drooping. Seeds are cottony.

Leaves are triangular, leathery, glossy, to 7" wide, with long stalks (to 5"), truncated bases, pointed tips, and toothed margins.

Found along roads, canals, streams, and rivers.

Life Zones: Plains and Foothills

Flowering Time: April to June

Bluestem Willow

Salix irrorata

Willow Family (Salicaceae)

Shrub, to 12' high, with straight, darkgray stems and bluish twigs.

Flowers are arranged in catkins, male and female on the same tree. Male catkins are hairy, to ¾" long; female catkins are smooth, to 1½" long.

Leaves are alternate, dark green, to 5" long, and hairy beneath.

Grows along streams and rivers.

Life Zone: Foothills

Flowering Time: April and May

Peachleaf Willow

Salix amygdaloides

Willow Family (Salicaceae)

Tree, to 40' tall, or shrub, with many stems and drooping, yellowish branchlets.

Male catkins are less than 2" long; female catkins to 3".

Leaves are narrow and lance-shaped, to 6" long, shiny and dark green on top, and grayish beneath, with toothed margins.

Grows in wet places, such as swamps, ditches, pond shores, and stream banks.

Life Zones: Plains to Montane

Flowering Time: April and May

Sandbar Willow

(Coyote Willow)

Salix exigua
(S. interior)

Willow Family (Salicaceae)

Shrub, to 8' tall, with slender, yellow, reddish, and tannish branches.

Male flowers are in ascending, 1¼" long, woolly catkins. Female flowers in silky, 1½" long, drooping clusters.

Leaves are alternate, to 5" long, hairy, and slender.

Grows in moist areas, such as river and stream banks, sandy or gravelly floodplains, and ditches.

Life Zones: Plains and Foothills

Flowering Time: May and June

Rough Pigweed

(Green Amaranth, Wild Beet, Redroot)

Amaranthus retroflexus

Amaranth Family
(Amaranthaceae)

Stout annual, to 4' high, with several hairy stems.

Flowers are tiny, green, and arranged in spikes that are grouped in panicles.

Leaves are alternate, ovate, tapering at both ends, about 3" long, and stalked.

European import that likes dumps, waste places, fields, roadsides, and cultivated ground.

Life Zones: Plains to Montane

Flowering Time:
August to October

Giant Ragweed

(Buffaloweed)

Ambrosia trifida

Aster Family (Asteraceae)

Annual, to 8' tall, with erect, rough stems, oppositely branched.

Flower heads are segregated by sex. The male heads are saucer-shaped, yellowish green, drooping in spike-like racemes; female heads are clustered in leaf axils and subtended by a pair of 3-lobed bracts.

Leaves are opposite and deeply cleft into 3 or 5 ovate, toothed lobes.

Abundant in disturbed and waste areas, such as fields, roadsides, and vacant lots.

Life Zone: Plains

Flowering Time: June to September

Western Ragweed
Ambrosia psilostachya coronopifolia

Aster Family (Asteraceae)

Perennial, with horizontal rootstock, to 5' tall, with erect, many-branched, hairy stems.

Flower heads are small, segregated by sex on the same spikelike raceme, with male flower heads at the top and female flower heads below, subtended by bristly, leafy bracts.

Leaves are deeply cut into narrow leaflets that are lobed and hairy beneath.

Common on roadsides, vacant lots, fields, and pastures.

Life Zone: Plains

Flowering Time: July to October

Common Cattail

(Broad-Leaved Cattail, Cattail Flag,
 Reed Mace)

Typha latifolia

Cattail Family (Typhaceae)

Perennial, to 10' tall, in dense patches, with erect, unbranched stem.

Flowers are in terminal spike. The male flowers are at the tip of the stem and disappear after shedding their pollen; female flowers form a brown, sausagelike spike below the male spike.

Leaves are longer than the stem, flat, 1" wide, and tough.

Common in wet places, such as ponds, lakeshores, marshes, and ditches.

Life Zones: Plains and Foothills

Flowering Time: May to August

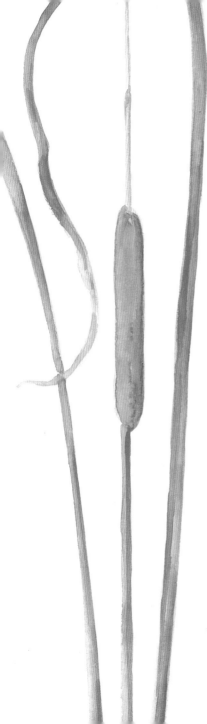

Narrowleaved Cattail

(Nailrod)

Typha angustifolia

Cattail Family (Typhaceae)

Perennial, to 6' tall, in dense stands, with round, smooth stem.

Flowers are in terminal spikes. Male flowers are at the tip and are shed early; female flowers appear about 2" below the male spike. Spikes are sausagelike, tannish brown, velvety, to 5½" long and ⅝" wide.

Leaves are taller than the stem, narrow (¼" wide), convex beneath, and flat on top.

Grows in shallow water, wet ditches, seeps, and pond edges.

Life Zones: Plains to Montane

Flowering Time: May and June

Green Goosefoot

Chenopodium atrovirens
(C. wolfii, C. aridum)

Goosefoot Family (Chenopodiaceae)

Annual, to 32" tall, with erect, striped, angular stem.

Flowers are tiny ($^1/_{16}$"), with green and white sepals, in tight, round clusters that make up spikelike panicles. The fruit is round and purplish black.

Leaves are alternate, to 2" long, elliptical to ovate, stalked, and dark green above.

Grows along roads, in fields, and on disturbed ground and hillsides.

Life Zones: Plains to Montane

Flowering Time: July to September

Lamb's Quarter

(Common Pigweed)

Chenopodium album
(C. hians)

Goosefoot Family
(Chenopodiaceae)

Annual, to 2' tall, smelly, with erect stem covered with mealy powder.

Flowers are small, without petals, in dense clusters that make up branched, mealy powdered spikes.

Leaves are mealy beneath, triangular, thick, with pointed lobes.

Common in yards and fields, and on vacant lots and roadsides.

Life Zone: Plains

Flowering Time: July to October

Saltbush

(Saltbrush)

Atriplex heterosperma

Goosefoot Family (Chenopodiaceae)

Annual, to 3' high, with ribbed, hairless, branched stem.

Flowers are inconspicuous, without petals or sepals. Female flowers are enclosed by 2 green, ovate bracts. Male flowers consist only of 5 stamens. Seeds are flat, ovate, 2-winged on one side, $^3/_{16}$" long, and prominently veined.

Leaves are triangular, with widely spaced teeth, and blades to 6" long on 1½" long stalks.

Grows on disturbed ground along roads, streams, and the edges of fields. Eurasian immigrant.

Life Zone: Plains

Flowering Time: July to September

Virginia Creeper

(Woodbine)

Parthenocissus quinquefolia

Grape Family (Vitaceae)

Perennial woody vine, with tendrils that have adhesive pads.

Flowers are greenish, in flat-topped clusters, with 5 thick petals that drop off. Berries are dark blue, ¼" wide, on fleshy, red stalks.

Leaves are lobed into 5 or 7 coarse-toothed leaflets.

Climbs rocky slopes, walls, trees, riverbanks, and fences.

Life Zone: Plains

Flowering Time: June to August

Blue Grama

(Grama Grass)

Chondrosum gracile
(Bouteloua gracilis, B. oligostachya)

Grass Family (Poaceae)

Tufted perennial, to 2' tall, with slender, erect stem.

Flowers are in spikelets, ¼" long. As many as 80 spikelets are crowded into one-sided, 1½" long spikes.

Leaves are curled, ³⁄₃₂" wide, and up to 6" long.

Common in sandy soils on hillsides and prairie slopes. Blue Grama is the state grass of Colorado.

Life Zones: Plains to Montane

Flowering Time: July to September

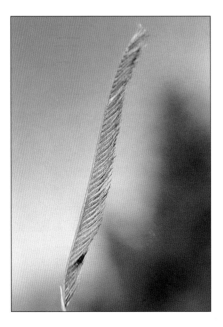

Downy Brome

(Down Bromegrass)

Anisantha tectorum
(Bromus tectorum)

Grass Family (Poaceae)

Tufted annual, to 2' tall, upright or spreading.

Flowers form spikelets with ¾" awns. Spikelets form drooping, 6", reddish purple panicles.

Leaves are soft, hairy, and about ¼" wide.

Common in waste areas and fields, on hillsides, and along roads.

Life Zones: Plains to Montane

Flowering Time: May and June

Poverty Brome

(Cheat Grass)

Anisantha sterilis
(Bromus sterilis)

Grass Family (Poaceae)

Annual, to 3' tall, tufted, with erect stems.

Flowers have 1" long, barbed awns, in ⅜" spikelets that form a drooping panicle.

Leaves are rough, hairy, and ³⁄₁₆" wide.

Grows in fields and pastures, along roads, and in waste places.

Life Zones: Plains and Foothills

Flowering Time: April to July

Crabgrass

(Hairy Crabgrass, Fingergrass)

Digitaria sanguinalis
(Syntherisma sanguinalis)

Grass Family (Poaceae)

Annual, to 3' high, rooting at the nodes.

Flowers are ⅛" long, in paired spikelets, on one-sided, slender, fingerlike spikes.

Leaves are lax, to 6" long, and ⅜" wide.

Weedy pest, grows in lawns, fields, and roadsides.

Life Zones: Plains and Foothills

Flowering Time: July to September

Barnyard Grass

Echinochloa crus-galli

Grass Family (Poaceae)

Annual, to 5' high, branching at base, with fleshy, smooth stem.

Flowers in crowded, purplish green, bristly, spikelets that make up the branches of a brushlike panicle, that can be up to 10" long.

Leaves are ⅝" wide and to 20" long, with bristly margins.

Common in gardens, farmyards, ditches, and pastures.

Life Zone: Plains

Flowering Time:
July to November

Buffalo Grass

Buchloë dactyloides
(Bulbilis dactyloides)

Grass Family (Poaceae)

Perennial, to 10" tall, with long runners rooting at the nodes. Forms large patches and sod.

Male and female flowers are segregated on separate plants. Male flowers are in flaglike, one-sided spikes; female flowers are hidden in spikelets that are enclosed by egglike structures and obscured by leaves near the ground.

Leaves are short (to 4" long), flat, curly, and grayish.

Grows in dry places on hillsides and prairie slopes.

Life Zone: Plains

Flowering Time: May to August

Orchard Grass

Dactylis glomerata

Grass Family (Poaceae)

Perennial, to 4' tall, in clumps, with erect, smooth stems.

Flowers are in short-awned spikelets that form clusters on the stiff branches of a 6" long panicle.

Leaves are bluish green and bristly, to ¼" wide and 20" long.

Grows in lawns, fields, orchards, open woods, and along roadsides.

Life Zone: Plains

Flowering Time: May to August

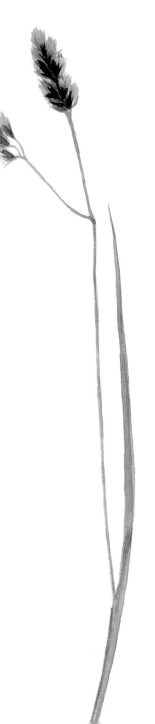

Windmill Grass

Chloris verticillata

Grass Family (Poaceae)

Perennial, to 18" high, tufted, rooting at the nodes, with erect or leaning stem.

Flowers are in ⅛", awned spikelets. These form stiff, spreading, reddish, slender spikes (to 6" long) that make up the panicle.

Leaves are pale, ⅛" wide, and have blunt tips.

Grows in disturbed areas in fields and on the prairies.

Life Zone: Plains

Flowering Time: June to October

Green Bristlegrass

(Green Foxtail)

Setaria viridis
(Chaetochloa viridis)

Grass Family (Poaceae)

Annual, to 3' high, with erect stems branching at base.

Flowers are in small (⅛") spikelets, flattened, green and/or purplish, with barbed bristles; spikelets are arranged in a cylindrical panicle.

Leaves are flat, to 6" long and ⅜" wide, with rough margins.

Very common in fields, disturbed areas, and cultivated plots.

Life Zone: Plains

Flowering Time: July to October

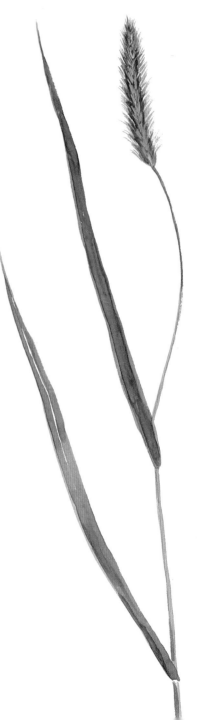

Kentucky Bluegrass

Poa pratensis

Grass Family (Poaceae)

Perennial, to 3' tall, with slender, wiry stem and long rootstock. Grows in tufts.

Flowers are in ¼" long spikelets, making up a pyramidal, open panicle.

Leaves are bright green, ⅛" wide, and flat, with blunt tips.

Grows in open waste areas, in lawns and pastures, and along roads.

Life Zone: Plains

Flowering Time: May to July

Rye

Secale cereale

Grass Family (Poaceae)

Annual, to 6' tall, with erect, slender, smooth stem.

Flowers have 3" long, stiff awns, and are in 2-flowered spikelets that make up an erect, 3" spike.

Leaves are narrow (to ¼" wide), flat, papery, and reflexed.

Escapee from cultivation; found along roads and in fallow fields and waste places.

Life Zone: Plains

Flowering Time: June to August

Canada Wild Rye

(Canada Ryegrass)

Elymus canadensis

Grass Family (Poaceae)

Perennial, to 5' tall; tufted, with erect to arching, bluish stem.

Flowers have 1" long awns and form 10" long, nodding spikes.

Leaves to 12" long and ⅝" wide, hard, rough on top.

Grows in dry, open areas on sandy hillsides and rocky slopes, in open woods, and prairies.

Life Zones: Plains and Foothills

Flowering Time:
July to September

Tall Wheatgrass

(Slender Wheatgrass)

Lophopyrum elongatum
(Elytrigia elongata,
Agropyron elongatum)

Grass Family (Poaceae)

Perennial bunch grass, to 10' high, with smooth, hard, dark green stem.

Flowers are in long spikes (to 12"), with ¾" spikelets that have blunt, ⅜" glumes.

Leaves to ¼" wide, with long sheaths and raspy margins.

Grows along roads and in vacant lots and fields. European native imported to stabilize soil.

Life Zone: Plains

Flowering Time: July to October

Wild Hops

Humulus lupulus americanus

Mulberry Family (Moraceae)

Perennial vine, to 20' long.

Male and female flowers are on separate plants. Male flowers are clustered and hang from leaf axils; female flowers are cone-shaped, green, papery spikelets.

Leaves are lobed into 3 or 5 toothed leaflets.

Grows in gardens and in open woods; climbs on other plants or hedges.

Life Zones: Plains and Foothills

Flowering Time: July to September

Curly Dock

(Yellow Dock, Narrow-Leaved Dock)

Rumex crispus

Knotweed Family (Polygonaceae)

Perennial, to 5' tall, with erect, grooved, hairless stem.

Flowers are small and crowded in whorls, on long clusters. Fruit is winged.

Leaves to 12" long, mostly basal, with wavy margins.

Common in moist areas in fields, waste ground, and gardens.

Life Zones: Plains and Foothills

Flowering Time: June to September

Stinging Nettle
(Common Nettle)

Urtica gracilis
(U. dioica)

Nettle Family (Urticaceae)

Perennial, with erect stem (to 6' high) and creeping root.

Flowers are small, brownish green, in spikelike racemes. Male flower is erect and has sepals only (4); female flower droops and has 2 petals.

Leaves are opposite, to 6" long, toothed, dark green, and hairless on top, with stinging hairs beneath.

Found in damp areas of woods and thickets, in river bottoms, and along roads and streams.

Life Zones:
Plains to Montane

Flowering Time:
July to September

51

Common Plantain

Plantago major

Plantain Family (Plantaginaceae)

Perennial, to 16" tall, with shiny stems that are erect but curved.

Flowers are ⅛" long, with 4 waxy, green sepals and 4 papery, tannish petals. Flowers grow in long (to 5") spikes.

Leaves are basal, to 4" long and 2" wide, thick, with wavy margins.

Grows on trails, along roads, in lawns and fields.

Life Zone: Plains

Flowering Time: June to October

English Plantain

(Buckhorn, Ribgrass)

Plantago lanceolata

Plantain Family (Plantaginaceae)

Perennial, to 30" tall, with rootstock and slender, tough, grooved stems.

Flowers are crowded into cylindrical spikes. They have a cup-shaped calyx, 4 papery, tannish petals, and long, protruding, white stamens.

Leaves are basal, to 16" long, narrow, with long stalks.

Common in grassy areas, along roads and trails, and in lawns.

Life Zone: Plains

Flowering Time: April to October

Great Bulrush

(Roundstem Bulrush,
 Clubrush, Hardstem
 Bulrush, Tule Bulrush)

Schoenoplectus lacustris acutus
(Scirpus lacustris, S. acutus,
 S. occidentalis)

Sedge Family (Cyperaceae)

Perennial, to 10' tall, with
creeping rootstock and stiff,
round, dark green stem.
Grows in patches.

Flowers are in brown spikelets
grouped into ¾" long clusters.

Leaves are round, to 16" long.

Common in shallow streams and
ponds, mud and seepage areas.

Life Zones: Plains and Foothills

Flowering Time: June to August

Pale Bulrush

Scirpus pallidus
(S. atrovirens)

Sedge Family (Cyperaceae)

Perennial, to 4' tall, with short rootstock and triangular, stout, light-green stem.

Flowers form grayish brown spikelets, grouped into spikes that form tight, ¾" clusters. Subtending scales are blackish and awned.

Leaves are grasslike, to ⅝" wide, with brownish sheaths and bristly margins and midveins.

Common in wet meadows, ditches, and marshes, and along the edges of lakes and ponds.

Life Zones: Plains and Foothills

Flowering Time: July and August

Small-Fruited Bulrush

Scirpus microcarpus
(S. rubrotinctus)

Sedge Family (Cyperaceae)

Perennial, to 4' tall, with runners and stout, smooth, triangular stem.

Flowers are in ⅛" spikes grouped into ¾" clusters.

Leaves are firm, ½" wide, extending beyond the flowers.

Grows in wet places, such as pond shores, marshes, meadows, sloughs, and ditches.

Life Zones: Plains and Foothills

Flowering Time: July and August

Soft-Stem Bulrush

(Tule, Great Bulrush)

Schoenoplectus lacustris creber
(Scirpus lacustris, S. validus)

Sedge Family (Cyperaceae)

Perennial, to 10' tall, with creeping rootstock and soft, round stem.

Flowers are in reddish brown spikelets arranged in elongate, drooping clusters.

Leaves are absent except for a stiff blade at the tip of the stem.

Grows in wet places, such as ditches, pond shores, riverbanks, and mudflats.

Life Zone: Plains

Flowering Time: June to August

Emory's Sedge

Carex emoryi
(C. stricta emoryi,
C. virginiana elongata)

Sedge Family (Cyperaceae)

Perennial, to 40" tall, in tufts, with long, horizontal rootstock and erect, stout stems.

Flowers are in spikes. The upper spikes (to 1¾" long) are all male, whereas the lower spikes are either male or female.

Leaves, 4 per stem, are ³⁄₁₆" wide and flat or inrolled.

Grows in wet places, such as meadows, swamps, stream banks, ditches, and springs.

Life Zone: Plains

Flowering Time: April to June

Thread-Leaved Sedge

Carex filifolia

Sedge Family (Cyperaceae)

Perennial, to 10" high, tufted, forming dense tussocks, with stout rootstock and threadlike, wiry stems.

Flowers form one erect spike, to 1¼" long. Spike's upper part is male (without bracts); lower part is female, with up to 15 bracts hidden by broad, hyaline scales.

Leaves are threadlike, stiff, and wiry.

Common along ridges and on dry prairies, grassy slopes, sage flats, and floodplains.

Life Zones: Plains to Foothills

Flowering Time: April to June

Banana Yucca

(Datil Yucca, Datil, Indian Banana, Blue Yucca)

Yucca baccata

Agave Family (Agavaceae)

Shrub with stout, branching rootstock, short, woody stems, and 5' high flower stalk.

Flowers, in drooping clusters, form a panicle. Flowers are bell-shaped, to 4" long, with 3 white, waxy petals and 3 waxy, white to purplish sepals. The fruit is fleshy, cylindrical, to 10" long, and edible.

Leaves are evergreen, basal, thick, and rigid, to 3' long and 2" wide, bluish green, with fibrous, curled margins.

Grows in southern and western Colorado, in deserts, prairie, and chapparal, and on rocky slopes and ledges.

Life Zones: Plains to Foothills

Flowering Time: April to July

Yucca

(Soapweed, Spanish Bayonet)

Yucca glauca

Agave Family (Agavaceae)

Shrub with stout rootstock, short, woody stems, and 5' high flower stalks.

Flowers are bell-shaped, to 4" long, with 3 white petals and 3 brownish sepals, and are arranged in drooping clusters on a narrow panicle. The fruit is podlike and dry.

Leaves are basal, evergreen, to 30" long and less than ½" wide, sharp, with frayed margins.

Grows in dry areas, in deserts and on prairie slopes and hillsides.

Life Zones: Plains to Foothills

Flowering Time: May to July

61

Redroot

(New Jersey Tea)

Ceanothus herbaceus

Buckthorn Family
(Rhamnaceae)

Shrub, to 2' high, erect or creeping, with smooth, greenish gray twigs.

Flowers are white, tiny (¹⁄₁₆"), in crowded clusters.

Leaves are alternate, narrowly ovate, to 2" long, green on top, and soft and hairy beneath.

Grows in sandy soil on hillsides and mesas, and in open woods.

Life Zones:
Plains and Foothills

Flowering Time:
June to August

Red-Osier Dogwood

(Redstemmed Cornel)

Swida sericea
(Cornus sericea, C. stolonifera)

Dogwood Family (Cornaceae)

Shrub with several stems, to 8' high, and with smooth, red branchlets.

Flowers are tiny (less than ¼"), white, and grow in flat-topped clusters. Berries are small and white—sometimes bluish or grayish.

Leaves are opposite and oval, with pointed tips and entire margins, to 4" long.

Grows in moist, shady areas, such as bogs, meadows, and stream banks.

Life Zones: Plains to Subalpine

Flowering Time:
May to August

Winterfat

(White Sage)

Krascheninnikovia lanata
(Ceratoides lanata, Eurotia lanata)

Goosefoot Family
(Chenopodiaceae)

Shrub, to 3' tall, with whitish, woolly branches; grows in patches.

Flowers are small, in spikes. Male and female flowers are on separate plants.

Leaves are whorled, thick, to 1½" long, with curled margins.

Grows in dry environments, such as sunny slopes, sandy plains, and alkali flats.

Life Zones: Plains to Foothills

Flowering Time: June to August

Kinnikinnik

(Bearberry)

Arctostaphylos uva-ursi
(A. adenotricha)

Heath Family (Ericaceae)

Shrub, to 6" high, creeping and mat-forming.

Flowers are urn-shaped and white with pinkish tips; they form short clusters. Berries, to ⅜" across, are bright red when mature.

Leaves are evergreen, to 1" long, oblong, spatulate, shiny, and leathery.

Grows in dry, exposed areas, such as sandy and rocky slopes, hillsides, and open conifer woods.

Life Zones:
Foothills to Subalpine

Flowering Time: April to June

Fly Honeysuckle

(Red Twinberry, Morrow's Honeysuckle,
 Utah Honeysuckle)

Lonicera morrowii
(L. utahensis)

Honeysuckle Family (Caprifoliaceae)

Shrub, to 10' tall, with diverging
branches and light gray, shedding
bark.

Flowers are paired and stalked,
with white to yellowish, ¾" long
petals and hairy calyx. Berries are
bright red to yellowish and paired.

Leaves are opposite, leathery, with
pointed tips and hairy margins.

Common in thickets and along
roads and the edges of woods.

Life Zones: Plains to Foothills

Flowering Time: June to August

Snowberry

(Wolfberry, Buckbrush, Western Snowberry)

Symphoricarpos occidentalis

Honeysuckle Family (Caprifoliaceae)

Shrub, to 5' tall, in dense colonies, with slender, whitish twigs.

Flowers are in terminal and axillary clusters, with 5 reflexed, white lobes that have pinkish tinge; the 5 stamens and pistil protrude, and the corolla is bell-shaped, to ⅜" high. Berries are whitish and about ⁵⁄₁₆" in diameter.

Leaves are oval, to 4" long, opposite, and grayish beneath.

Grows in moist places, in ravines and along rivers and streams.

Life Zones: Plains to Montane

Flowering Time: June to August

Snowball Tree

(Guelder Rose)

Viburnum opulus

Honeysuckle Family
(Caprifoliaceae)

Shrub, to 15' tall, with tannish gray bark and smooth, reddish twigs.

Flowers in large umbels, to 6" across. Outer flowers are large (to ¾") but sterile; the fertile inner flowers are small and inconspicuous. Berries are orange to red, juicy but bitter.

Leaves are opposite and palmately divided into 3 or 5, toothed lobes.

Escaped from cultivation to fence rows, edges of woods, and stream banks.

Life Zones:
Plains and Foothills

Flowering Time:
May to July

Wayfaring Tree

(Twistwood)

Viburnum lantana

Honeysuckle Family
(Caprifoliaceae)

Shrub or small tree, to 15' tall, with opposite branches and gray, felty twigs.

Flowers are white, in clusters that make up 3" wide umbels.

Leaves are opposite, to 5" long, densely hairy beneath.

Escaped from cultivation to roadsides, fence rows, and gulches.

Life Zones:
Plains and Foothills

Flowering Time:
May and June

Waxflower

(Cliffbush, Mountain Mock Orange,
 Jamesia)

Jamesia americana

Hydrangea Family (Hydrangeaceae)

Small shrub, to 5' high, with stiff
branches and peeling bark.

Flowers are in small clusters;
the 5 petals are white, waxy,
to ½" long.

Leaves are opposite, to 2⅜"
long, dark green above and
velvety white beneath, and
heart-shaped.

Grows on rocky slopes and
steep canyon walls, in crevices,
and on cliffs.

Life Zones: Foothills to Subalpine

Flowering Time: May to July

Black Locust

(False Acacia)

Robinia pseudoacacia

Pea Family (Fabaceae)

Tree or shrub, to 50' tall, with grayish brown, fissured bark, odd-angled branching, and sticky twigs with thorns.

Flowers to 4" long, with 2-lipped white corolla, in drooping, one-sided racemes to 4" long. The seed pods are slender and flat, to 4" long.

Leaves are pinnately compound, divided into 2" long leaflets.

Escapee from cultivation to roadsides, ditches, and fence rows.

Life Zone: Plains

Flowering Time: May and June

Apache Plume

(Feather Rose)

Fallugia paradoxa

Rose Family (Rosaceae)

Erect shrub, to 5' high, much branched, with slender, whitish twigs.

Flowers to 1½" across, with white petals. Fruits have feathery plumes.

Leaves are small (to 1" long) and cut into several linear lobes.

Grows on exposed slopes, canyon sides, and prairies of southern Colorado.

Life Zones:
Plains to Montane

Flowering Time:
May to October

Arkansas Rose

(Wild Prairie Rose, Wild Rose)

Rosa arkansana

Rose Family (Rosaceae)

Shrub, to 2' tall, with bristly, creeping or leaning stems that die back.

Flowers are large (to 3") and grow in clusters, with 5 white or pinkish petals. The fruit (hip) is red, ellipsoid, and up to ⅝" long.

Leaves are pinnately divided into 5 to 7 toothed leaflets.

Grows in thickets, on slopes and hillsides, and along ditches and railroad embankments.

Life Zones: Plains and Foothills

Flowering Time: June and July

Common Shadbush

(Smooth Shadbush, Serviceberry,
Saskatoon Serviceberry, Juneberry,
Sugarplum)

Amelanchier alnifolia
(A. pumila)

Rose Family (Rosaceae)

Small tree or shrub, to 12'
tall; creates thickets from
underground stems.

Flowers are stalked and in
clusters, with 5 slender, white
petals. Berries are ½" across,
dark purple, juicy, and edible.

Leaves are alternate, to 2½"
long, broadly oval, pale, and
downy beneath.

Grows along streams and
forest edges, in clearings,
and on hillsides.

Life Zones:
Plains to Subalpine

Flowering Time:
April to June

Firethorn

Cotoneaster pyracantha
(Pyracantha coccinea)

Rose Family (Rosaceae)

Shrub, to 8' tall, much branched, leafy, and spiny.

Flowers are small (to ⅜"), in clusters, with 5 white, spoon-shaped petals. Fruit is berrylike, bright orange, and persistent.

Leaves are evergreen, leathery, shiny, with blunt-toothed margins.

Escapee from cultivation to roadsides, thickets, and ditches.

Life Zone: Plains

Flowering Time: May and June

Boulder Raspberry

(Rocky Mountain Thimbleberry,
 Flowering Raspberry)

Oreobatus deliciosus
(Rubus deliciosus)

Rose Family (Rosaceae)

Shrub, to 5' tall, with arching
branches and shredded, tannish
bark.

Flowers are showy, to 3" wide,
with 5 white petals. Berries
are about ⅜" across, pinkish
or purplish, and tasteless—
not "delicious," as the Latin
name implies.

Leaves are simple, palmately
lobed, bright green on top,
with toothed margins.

Grows in sunny, open areas,
such as hillsides and rocky
slopes, and along roads and
the edges of woods.

Life Zones: Plains to Montane

Flowering Time: June and July

Red Raspberry

(Wild Red Raspberry,
 American Red Raspberry)

Rubus idaeus melanolasius

Rose Family (Rosaceae)

Rambling shrub, to 6' tall, forming thickets via suckers, with slender, bristly branches.

Flowers are in small clusters, with 5 white petals and 5 sticky, reflexed sepals. Berries are red, to ½" across, and delicious.

Leaves are alternate and divided into as many as 7 sharply toothed leaflets that are white beneath.

Prefers moist, cool sites in forests and gulches; also found along roads and on hillsides.

Life Zones:
Foothills to Subalpine

Flowering Time:
July and August

Shiny-Leaved Hawthorn
(Redstemmed Hawthorn,
 Cerro Hawthorn)
Crataegus erythropoda
Rose Family (Rosaceae)

Tree or shrub, to 15' tall,
with shiny, brownish red
twigs and purplish thorns.

Flowers are saucer-shaped,
to ¾" across, white, and in
clusters. Fruit is brownish
purple and small (to ¼").

Leaves are alternate,
to 3" long, dark green,
hairless, and sharply
toothed.

Found in moist areas
in canyons, on hillsides,
and along streams.

Life Zones:
Plains to Montane

Flowering Time:
May and June

Western Chokecherry

(Black Chokecherry)

Padus virginiana melanocarpa

Rose Family (Rosaceae)

Tall shrub or small, spreading tree, to 20' high, forming thickets, with reddish brown bark marked by lenticels (horizontal fissures).

Flowers are in drooping, sausage-like clusters, to 6" long. Cherries are shiny, dark red to black, and about ⅜" in diameter.

Leaves are alternate, to 4" long, elliptical, with pointed tips and finely toothed margins.

Common in moist areas along streams, on hillsides, and in gulches and canyons.

Life Zones: Plains to Montane

Flowering Time: May and June

Wild Plum

(American Plum)

Prunus americana

Rose Family (Rosaceae)

Shrub or small tree, to 8' tall, in dense thickets, with grayish bark and stiff branches.

Flowers are fragrant, in loose clusters, with 5 waxy, white petals and 5 green to reddish, reflexed sepals. Fruit is yellow, red, or purple, to 1" long, with flattened pits.

Leaves are finely toothed and taper to a point.

Grows in moist areas in canyons and gulches, and along streams and irrigation ditches.

Life Zones:
Plains and Foothills

Flowering Time:
March to May

Poison Ivy

(Poison Oak)

Toxicodendron rydbergia
(T. radicans, Rhus radicans, R. toxicodendron)

Sumac Family (Anacardiaceae)

Shrub, to 2' high, with aerial rootlets and slender twigs. Grows in large patches.

Flowers are small (¼"), inconspicuous, in dense clusters, with creamy white petals. Berries are yellowish white, to ⅜" across, and shiny.

Leaves are alternate, divided into 3 ovate, shiny leaflets that turn red in autumn.

Grows along roadsides, railroad tracks, and stream banks, and in waste places and gulches. *Poisonous:* causes skin rash, as I know well.

Life Zones: Plains and Foothills

Flowering Time: May and June

Smooth Sumac

(Rocky Mountain Sumac)

Rhus glabra

Sumac Family (Anacardiaceae)

Shrub or small tree, to 8' tall, forming thickets, with stout, erect or spreading stems and smooth, reddish twigs.

Flowers are segregated by sex on different trees. Male flowers are grouped in 12" long, loose panicles; female flowers are in dense, 6" long panicles, with greenish white petals. Berries are ³⁄₁₆" long, sticky, and hairy.

Leaves are alternate, to 12" long, and pinnately divided into many pairs of leaflets. Leaflets are dark green and shiny on top, silvery beneath, and have toothed margins.

Grows in dry, sandy soil along roads and on hillsides, ridges, and rocky slopes.

Life Zones: Plains and Foothills

Flowering Time: June to August

Many-Flowered Aster

Virgulus ericoides
(Aster ericoides, A. multiflorus)

Aster Family (Asteraceae)

Perennial, to 2' tall, with erect, twisted, rough, shiny, and woody stems.

Flower heads crowded in one-sided clusters, with white or pinkish ray flowers and 3 tiers of bracts.

Leaves are linear, to 2½" long, rough, and rather stiff.

Grows on dry ground along roads and fences, on sandy hillsides, and in openings in woods.

Life Zones: Plains and Foothills

Flowering Time: July to October

Rough White Aster

Virgulus falcatus
(Aster falcatus, A. commutatus)

Aster Family (Asteraceae)

Perennial, to 4' tall, in patches, with horizontal rootstock and woody, wiry, hairy stems.

Flower heads are many, small (½"), bunched in one-sided racemes, with white ray flowers and slender, reflexed, bristly bracts.

Leaves are narrow, to 3" long, thick and twisted, bristly beneath.

Abundant along roads and fence rows, in fields and meadows, and on embankments and slopes.

Life Zones: Plains and Foothills

Flowering Time: July to October

Blackfoot Daisy
(White Paper Flower, Rock Daisy,
 Mountain Daisy, Plains Blackfoot)

Melampodium leucanthum

Aster Family (Asteraceae)

Perennial, to 16" high, woody
at base, and much-branched.

Flower heads to 1½" across,
with broad, white to pinkish
ray flowers.

Leaves are opposite, narrow,
hairy, sticky, and sometimes
lobed.

Grows in rocky, gravelly places,
such as desert, hillsides, slopes,
outcrops, and ledges.

Life Zones: Plains and Foothills

Flowering Time:
March to October

Easter Daisy

(Stemless Daisy, Early Townsendia)

Townsendia hookeri

Aster Family (Asteraceae)

Perennial, with stout taproot and no stem.

Flower heads are large (1" across), with white or pinkish ray flowers in tiers, and hairy bracts.

Leaves are basal, slender, grayish, and densely hairy.

Grows in sunny, dry areas, such as sandy hillsides and gravelly or rocky slopes.

Life Zones: Plains and Foothills

Flowering Time: March to June

Low Daisy

(Early White Erigeron)

Erigeron pumilus pumilus

Aster Family (Asteraceae)

Perennial, to 10" high, in clumps, with woody rootstock and several sticky, hairy, branched stems.

Flower heads have many white to pinkish or purplish ray flowers and one row of sticky, hairy bracts.

Leaves are fleshy, to 2" long, twisted, sticky, and hairy.

Common in dry places, such as sandy hillsides, deserts, thickets, and mesas.

Life Zones: Plains and Foothills

Flowering Time: May to July

Oxeye Daisy

Leucanthemum vulgare
(Chrysanthemum leucanthemum)

Aster Family (Asteraceae)

Perennial, to 2' tall, with erect, grooved, unbranched stem.

Flower heads are large (to 3" across), with white ray flowers, yellow to orange disk, and bracts that form green, white, and brown saucers.

Leaves are alternate, to 6" long, deep green, and soft but hairless.

Common in open areas, such as fields and meadows, openings in woods, and along roads.

Life Zones: Plains to Montane

Flowering Time: May to October

Sprawling Daisy

Erigeron colo-mexicanus
(E. divergens cinereus, E. cinerius,
E. nudiflorus, E. commixtus)

Aster Family (Asteraceae)

Biennial, with long, slender, sprawling, leafy shoots and slender, leafless stems, to 10" high.

Flower heads are single (one per stem), to ¾" across, with many white rays that are pinkish beneath.

Leaves in basal cluster are spatulate, stalked, and up to 1½" long; leaves on shoots are linear, stalkless, about ½" long, and erect. All leaves are grayish and hairy.

Grows in dry areas on sandy, gravelly hillsides and in meadows.

Life Zones:
Plains and Foothills

Flowering Time:
March to August

Spreading Daisy

(Spreading Fleabane, Branching Daisy)

Erigeron divergens

Aster Family (Asteraceae)

Biennial, to 18" tall, much-branched from base, usually low and spreading, hairy.

Flower heads are many and small (to ¾" wide). Ray flowers (as many as 120 per head) are white, pale lavender, or pink; disk flowers are yellow; bracts are sticky and hairy.

Leaves to 2½" long and woolly.

Common in sandy or gravelly sites, such as roadsides, slopes, and open woods.

Life Zones: Plains to Montane

Flowering Time: April to September

European Milfoil

(Sneezeweed, Nosebleed Plant,
Common Yarrow, Chipmunk Tail,
Plumajill, Milfoil)

Achillea millefolium

Aster Family (Asteraceae)

Perennial, to 3½' tall, aromatic,
with stout, rough stems.

Flower heads are small
(¼"), white, and grouped in
umbrellalike clusters.

Leaves are feathery
and pinnately divided
into sharply lobed
leaflets.

Common in open
areas, such as road-
sides, fence rows,
fields, and meadows;
European import.

Life Zones:
Plains to Montane

Flowering Time:
May to October

Knapweed

(Tumble Knapweed)

Acosta diffusa
(Centaurea diffusa)

Aster Family (Asteraceae)

Annual or biennial,
to 3' tall, with rough,
stiff, much-branched
stems.

Flower heads are numerous,
small (to ¾"), in broad,
flat-topped panicles, with
narrow, cleft ray flowers
(white or purplish) and
spiny bracts.

Leaves are small
(to 1" long), rough,
and hairy; lower
leaves are lobed.

Grows on roadsides,
in fallow fields, on
disturbed ground, and
along ditches; European weed.

Life Zones: Plains and Foothills

Flowering Time: June to September

Showy Townsendia

(Showy Easter Daisy, Large-flowered Townsendia)

Townsendia grandiflora

Aster Family (Asteraceae)

Perennial, to 8" high, with stout taproot and erect, stout, whitish, hairy stems.

Flower heads are single, large (to 2" across), with white to pinkish or purplish ray flowers, greenish yellow disks, and tiered, slender, sharp, and bristly bracts.

Leaves are fleshy, thick, hairy to bristly, narrow, and up to 3" long.

Common on mesas, dry slopes and hillsides, and in thickets and open woods.

Life Zones: Plains and Foothills

Flowering Time: May to August

Bractless Cryptantha

Cryptantha crassisepala

Borage Family (Boraginaceae)

Annual, to 6" high, in clumps, with several gray, bristly, spreading stems.

Flowers are tiny (to ⅛"), in bractless spikes with 5 white petals.

Leaves are alternate, to 1" long, with long, stiff bristles.

Grows in dry areas, such as deserts, hillsides, and waste ground.

Life Zones: Plains and Foothills

Flowering Time: May and June

Miner's Candle

(Forget-Me-Not)

Oreocarya virgata
(Cryptantha virgata, C. spicata)

Borage Family (Boraginaceae)

Perennial or biennial, to 2' tall, with erect, unbranched, leafy, and bristly stem.

Flowers are small, in short, coiled clusters in axils; petals are pure white, waxy, and roundish.

Leaves are narrow, tough, and scratchy; they protrude between the flowers.

Abundant in dry areas, such as fields, sloping meadows, mesas, and canyon sides.

Life Zones: Plains to Montane

Flowering Time: May to July

White Clematis

(Western Virgin Bower,
 Peppervine, Pipestems)
Clematis ligusticifolia

Buttercup Family
(Ranunculaceae)

Vine, climbing and trailing,
with woody stems to 20' long.

Flowers are numerous,
without petals but with 4 or
5 petal-like sepals that are
white and reflexed. Male and
female flowers are on separate
plants. Fruits are one-seeded
and have long, silky hairs that
form fuzzy balls.

Leaves are opposite, divided
into 3 to 7 toothed leaflets.

Common in river bottoms,
along creeks, ditches, roads,
and fences, and in open
woods and thickets.

Life Zones: Plains and Foothills

Flowering Time:
May to September

Poison Hemlock

Conium maculatum

Celery Family (Apiaceae)

Biennial, to 10' tall, with stout taproot and hollow, ribbed stem that has purplish splotches.

Flowers are tiny and white, in 15 to 20 small clusters making up 1½" umbels, which combine into large clusters.

Leaves are fernlike, dissected into long-stalked and toothed leaflets.

Grows in moist environments, along streams, roads, and ditches; European immigrant. *Poisonous:* It killed Socrates.

Life Zones: Plains and Foothills

Flowering Time: July to August

Salt-and-Pepper

(Biscuitroot, Whiskbroom Parsley)

Lomatium orientale
(Cogswellia orientalis)

Celery Family (Apiaceae)

Perennial, to 12" tall, with short, leafless stem. One of the earliest bloomers.

Flowers are small (⅛"), with white petals and purplish bracts, in ¼" umbels that make up the main flower cluster.

Leaves are basal, with long stalks and blades that are divided into grayish green, soft, fleshy leaflets.

Common on grassy hillsides, on gravelly slopes, on mesas, and among outcrops.

Life Zones:
Plains and Foothills

Flowering Time:
March to June

Common Mouse-Ear

Cerastium fontanum
(C. vulgatum)

Chickweed Family (Alsinaceae)

Perennial, to 16" tall, with rooting, trailing stems, in clumps.

Flowers in open, loose clusters, with 5 white, deeply notched petals.

Leaves to 1½" long, with soft hairs.

Grows in disturbed areas, gardens, fields, and lawns.

Life Zones: Plains and Foothills

Flowering Time: May to July

Desert Sandwort

(Hooker Sandwort)

Eremogene hookeri
(Arenaria hookeri)

Chickweed Family (Alsinaceae)

Perennial, to 5" high, in tufts, with robust root; forms large patches.

Flowers are in tight clusters, with 5 white, waxy petals and 5 pointed, green and white sepals.

Leaves are opposite, to ¾" long, and linear.

Grows in dry areas, such as deserts, steppes, and chaparral, and on mesas and rocky slopes.

Life Zones: Plains and Foothills

Flowering Time: June and July

Indian Hemp

(Hemp Dogbane, Dogbane Hemp)

Apocynum cannabinum

Dogbane Family (Apocynaceae)

Perennial, to 3' tall, with opposite branching and erect, smooth stem.

Flowers are tiny, bell-shaped, greenish white, and in clusters. Seed pods are slender and up to 8" long.

Leaves are opposite, erect, hairy beneath, ovate, and up to 4" long.

Common in disturbed soil along roads and railroads, on hillsides, and in thickets and ditches.

Life Zone: Plains

Flowering Time: June to August

Prairie Evening Primrose

(Plains Evening Primrose)

Oenothera albicaulis

Evening Primrose Family
(Onagraceae)

Annual, to 18" high, in patches, with erect, pale, velvety stem.

Flowers are in loose cluster, with overlapping, white, 1" long petals that turn pink, and 4 white to pinkish sepals that bend back.

Leaves are alternate, deeply and pinnately incised, woolly, and grayish.

Grows in disturbed soils on sandy, barren slopes, along roads, and near anthills.

Life Zone: Plains

Flowering Time: May to July

Stemless Evening Primrose

(White Evening Primrose,
Morning Primrose, Fragrant
Morning Primrose, Rockrose,
Gumbu Primrose, Sandlily)

Oenothera caespitosa
(Pachylophus caespitosus)

Evening Primrose Family
(Onagraceae)

Perennial, short-stemmed,
to 8" high.

Flowers are large (to 4" across),
with 4 pure white petals that
turn orange.

Leaves are in basal rosette,
to 6" long, with toothed
to wavy margins.

Common on sunny hillsides,
slopes, and road cuts, in dry
prairies, and around anthills.

Life Zones: Plains to Montane

Flowering Time: May to August

Swamp Willowweed

Epilobium palustre grammadophyllum
(E. wyomingense)

Evening Primrose Family (Onagraceae)

Perennial, to 20" tall, with slender, erect stem.

Flowers are small (to $\frac{5}{16}$" long), on 2" stalks, with four white petals that can also be purplish or pinkish.

Leaves to 2¼" long, narrowly lance-shaped, and hairless.

Grows in wet meadows and thickets, near springs, and in bogs, swamps, and ditches.

Life Zones: Plains to Montane

Flowering Time: July to September

Blue-Eyed Mary

(Baby Blue-Eyes, Blue Eyes, Blue Lips)

Collinsia parviflora
(C. tenella)

Figwort Family (Scrophulariaceae)

Annual, to 10" tall (mostly 3"), with weak, slender stems.

Flowers are tiny (to ¼"), with white to pink, 2-lobed upper lip and blue to pink, 3-lobed lower lip. Calyx is goblet-shaped and reddish.

Leaves to 1" long, lance-shaped, opposite, fleshy, and hairless. Leaves are green above and red beneath.

Very common, but often overlooked, in shady places, such as openings in forests, hillsides and slopes, and disturbed areas.

Life Zones: Plains to Montane

Flowering Time: April to July

White Beardtongue

(White Penstemon)

Penstemon albidus
(P. teretiflorus, P. viscidulus)

Figwort Family (Scrophulariaceae)

Perennial, to 16" high, in tufts, with erect, purplish, sticky stem.

Flowers are 2-lipped; upper lip is 2-lobed, and lower lip is 3-lobed, white to purplish, and sticky.

Leaves are opposite, leathery, to 4" long; the lower leaves stalked.

Found at dry sites on hillsides.

Life Zones: Plains and Foothills

Flowering Time: May to July

Prairie Snowball

(Sand Verbena, Sweet Sand Verbena)

Abronia fragrans
(A. elliptica, A. glabra)

Four O'Clock Family (Nyctaginaceae)

Perennial, to 3' tall, with erect or sprawling, sticky, hairy stems.

Flowers are many, fragrant, and tubular, with 5 white to pinkish petals. Flowers form ball-like umbels.

Leaves are opposite, fleshy, to 3½" long, sticky, and hairy.

Grows in sand, in disturbed areas, and on prairie slopes.

Life Zones: Plains and Foothills

Flowering Time: May to August

Russian Tumbleweed

(Russian Thistle, Common Saltwort,
 Barillaplant)

Salsola australis
(S. iberica, S. pestifer, S. kali)

Goosefoot Family (Chenopodiaceae)

Annual, to 32" tall, bushy, with woody,
much-branched stem and stiff, striped
branches.

Flowers grow in leaf axils, with 5 papery,
white and pinkish petals and 3 spine-
tipped bracts.

Leaves are spine-tipped, to 2" long,
and straight.

Eurasian import; unwelcome but common
in dry, sandy environments, such as roadsides, fallow fields, and waste ground.

Life Zone: Plains

Flowering Time: July to September

Mock Cucumber

(Wild Cucumber, Wild Mock Cucumber,
Balsam Apple, Wild Balsam Apple)

Echinocyystis lobata
(Micrampelis lobata)

Gourd Family (Cucurbitaceae)

Annual vine, climbing and clinging, with smooth, angular stem
(to 20' long) and 3-forked tendrils.

Flowers are segregated on same plant.
Male flowers are greenish white, 2" long,
in elongate clusters; female flowers are
single. The seed pods are barrel-shaped,
to 2" long, and spiny.

Leaves are deeply lobed into 3 triangular
segments.

Grows on shrubs and small trees, on
fences, in waste places, on stream banks,
and along ditches.

Life Zones: Plains and Foothills

Flowering Time: June to October

White Larkspur

(Plains Larkspur)

Delphinium virescens penardii
(D. carolinianum penardii,
* D. camporum)*

Hellebore Family (Helleboraceae)

Perennial, to 4' tall, with erect, flexible, sticky, and hairy stems.

Flowers are 1" wide, with 5 white petaloid sepals—the uppermost of which is spurred—and 4 petals, with the upper 2 merging with the spur.

Leaves are palmately divided into stringlike lobes.

Grows in dry fields, on slopes and hillsides, and along roads.

Life Zones: Plains and Foothills

Flowering Time: May to July

Antelope Buckwheat

(James Buckwheat)

Eriogonum jamesii jamesii

Knotweed Family (Polygonaceae)

Perennial, to 12" tall, with erect, woolly, woody stem that has three sets of branches.

Flowers are small ($\frac{3}{16}$" high), white (sometimes greenish or pinkish), with protruding stamens; the small flower clusters are hairy and subtended by leaflike bracts.

Leaves are in basal rosette, to 4" long (including long stalk), leathery, woolly beneath.

Common on dry hillsides and in open woods and sloping fields in southern Colorado.

Life Zones: Plains to Montane

Flowering Time: July to September

Bushy Knotweed

Polygonum ramosissimum
(P. prolificum, P. rubescens)

Knotweed Family (Polygonaceae)

Annual, to 3' long, with slender, creeping stems.

Flowers are tiny, in small clusters, with white to pinkish petals.

Leaves are alternate, stalked, to 1½" long.

Common in disturbed and waste areas, such as roadsides, sidewalks, yards, and playgrounds.

Life Zone: Plains

Flowering Time: July to October

Mountain Knotweed

(Douglas Knotweed, Sawatch Knotweed)

Polygonum douglasii
(P. montanum, P. sawatchense)

Knotweed Family (Polygonaceae)

Annual, to 12" high, in colonies, with slender taproot and wiry, much-branched stem.

Flowers are tiny (³⁄₁₆" across), cup-shaped, with 5 white to pinkish corolla lobes.

Leaves are alternate, bright green, narrow (to ¼" wide), 1¾" long, stalkless, and pointed.

Common in dry areas of sage slopes, open woods, and mesas.

Life Zones: Plains to Subalpine

Flowering Time: June to August

Prairie Baby's Breath

(Bushy Eriogonum)

Eriogonum effusum

Knotweed Family
(Polygonaceae)

Perennial, to
12" tall, in clumps,
bushy, with wiry, reddish stems.

Flowers are small, in flat-topped
clusters, with bell-shaped, white corollas
and deltoid, green and pinkish bracts.

Leaves are mostly basal, 1½" long, narrow,
and hairy beneath.

Grows in dry areas on sunny slopes and
hillsides, and in disturbed soil and prairies.

Life Zones: Plains and Foothills

Flowering Time: July to September

Water Pepper

(Common Smartweed)

Persicaria hydropiper
(Polygonum hydropiper)

Knotweed Family
(Polygonaceae)

Annual, to 2' tall, with slender, erect or leaning stem.

Flowers are many, ⅛" long, with 5 white petals, and a green, white, and red calyx; flowers form tail-like racemes.

Leaves are narrowly lance-shaped, to 5" long, soft, with drawn-out tips.

Grows in wet areas, such as ditches, creeks, shores, and gullies.

Life Zone: Plains

Flowering Time:
June to October

Sand Lily

(Star Lily, Star-of-Bethlehem,
  Mountain Lily)

Leucocrinum montanum

Lily Family (Liliaceae)

Perennial, to 8" high, in clumps,
with vertical rootstock and no stems.

Flowers are tubular, with 6 white,
spreading tepals (undifferentiated
petals and sepals).

Leaves are linear, folded, to
8" long, and basal.

Grows in sand and clay on prairie
slopes, among sagebrush, and on
hillsides.

Life Zones: Plains and Foothills

Flowering Time: April to June

Goosegrass

(Bedstraw, Cleavers)

Galium spurium

Madder Family (Rubiaceae)

Annual, to 2' high or long, with stringlike root and slender, weak, angular, bristly stem that may be erect, spreading, or prostrate.

Flowers are tiny (¹⁄₁₆"), long-stalked, and form small clusters in leaf axils; they have 4 white and greenish petals. Fruits are bristly, to ³⁄₁₆" long.

Leaves are narrow, to 2" long, and bristly; in whorls of 8.

Grows along streams, on gravelly slopes, among shrubs, and in open woods; European import.

Life Zones: Plains to Montane

Flowering Time:
May to October

Common Mallow

(Cheeseweed)

Malva neglecta
(M. rotundifolia)

Mallow Family (Malvaceae)

Biennial, to 18" long, with taproot and creeping stem.

Flowers are ½" wide, in clusters, with 5 white to purplish petals. Fruit is divided into wedges.

Leaves are lobed, round in outline, and tend to fold into pleats.

Grows in waste places, such as dumps, fallow fields, and along roadsides, but also in lawns, yards, and gardens.

Life Zone: Plains

Flowering Time: May to October

False Solomon's Seal

(Claspleaf Solomon Plume, Solomon's Zigzag,
 False Spikeweed, Fat Solomonplume, Feather
 Solomonplume)

Maianthemum amplexicaule
(Smilacina amplexicaule, S. racemosa)

Mayflower Family (Convallariaceae)

Perennial, to 3' tall, with fleshy rootstock
and stout, leafy, smooth stem.

Flowers are tiny (⅛" long), with 3 white
petals and 3 white sepals, and arranged in
terminal clusters, to 6" long. The fruit is
berrylike, red, and ¼" long.

Leaves are large and broad, to 8" long, clasping, soft, with pointed tip and parallel veins.

Grows in shady spots in moist
woods, gullies, and thickets.

Life Zones: Plains and Foothills

Flowering Time: April to July

Antelope Horns

(Creeping Milkweed, Green-
Flowered Milkweed, Silkweed,
Spider Antelope Horns)

Asclepias asperula
(A. capricornu)

Milkweed Family
(Asclepiadaceae)

Perennial, to 2' tall, with
woody rootstock and stout,
erect, sticky, hairy, leafy stems.

Flowers are on 1" long, hairy
stalks, in terminal umbel, with
5 ovate, greenish white petals
that form reddish to purplish
hoods, and 5 short, sticky, hairy
sepals.

Leaves are alternate, to 6" long,
leathery, and grayish green.

Common in dry, sandy soils on
mesas and shrubby slopes, and
along roads.

Life Zones: Plains and Foothills

Flowering Time:
June to September

Dwarf Milkweed
(Low Milkweed)

Asclepias pumila

Milkweed Family
(Asclepiadaceae)

Perennial, to 8" high, with partially woody, erect, smooth stems.

Flowers are small and white, with reflexed lower petals and upper petals forming erect hoods.

Leaves are whorled, stringlike, to 2" long, smooth, and fleshy.

Grows in dry areas, on hillsides and mesas, and in open woods.

Life Zones: Plains and Foothills

Flowering Time: July to September

Catnip

Nepeta cataria

Mint Family (Lamiaceae)

Perennial, to 3' tall, with erect, branched, silky stem.

Flowers are clustered, with white, 2-lipped corolla and hairy, urn-shaped calyx.

Leaves are oval to heart-shaped, green above and whitish beneath, with long stalks.

Common along roads and in waste areas, pastures, gardens, and yards.

Life Zones:
Plains and Foothills

Flowering Time:
June to October

Common Horehound

(Horehound, White Horehound,
 Hoarhound)

Marrubium vulgare

Mint Family (Lamiaceae)

Perennial, to 2' tall, aromatic,
with erect, square, woolly stems.

Flowers are tiny, in dense clusters,
with 2-lipped corolla; the upper
lip is erect, and the lower lip is
spreading and 3-lobed.

Leaves are opposite, wrinkled,
woolly, and ovate.

Abundant in pastures, fields, and
roadsides.

Life Zone: Plains

Flowering Time: June to September

Bindweed

(Wild Morning Glory,
 Creeping Jenny, Small Bindweed,
 Possession Vine, Glorybind)

Convolvulus arvensis
(C. ambigens)

Morning Glory Family
(Convolvulaceae)

Perennial vine, to 8' long,
climbing, trailing, and
entwining, with tendrils.

Flowers are funnel-shaped,
white to pinkish, and 1" wide.

Leaves are arrow-shaped
and short-stalked.

European import;
a noxious weed that
grows in fields, lawns,
yards, and roadsides,
and on other plants,
fences, and posts.

Life Zone: Plains

Flowering Time:
May to October

Wild Morning Glory

(Hedge Bindweed)

Calystegia sepium angulata
(Convolvulus sepium, C. americanus,
C. interior, C. repens)

Morning Glory Family (Convolvulaceae)

Perennial vine, to 10' long, climbing, trailing, and entwining.

Flowers to 3" across, funnel-shaped, white, often in pairs, with 2 large bracts.

Leaves are arrow-shaped, narrow, and stalked.

Grows on hedges and fences, in thickets, on stream banks, and along canals and ditches.

Life Zone: Plains

Flowering Time: June to September

Hoary Alyssum

(False Alyssum)

Berteroa incana

Mustard Family (Brassicaeceae)

Annual (probably), to 2' tall, with hairy, leafy stems; grows in dense stands.

Flowers are small, in roundish clusters arranged in an elongate raceme; the 4 petals are white and cleft. Seed pods are hairy, oval, and flattened.

Leaves are hairy, grayish green, and lance-shaped.

Common in waste places, along roads and canals, and in meadows and fields.

Life Zones: Plains to Montane

Flowering Time:
May to November

Sweet Alyssum
Lobularia maritima

Mustard Family (Brassicaceae)

Annual, to 8" tall, with several slender stems that have whitish, V-shaped hairs.

Flowers are small, on spreading stalks, with 4 white and purple-tinged petals and ovate, hairy sepals. Pods are flat, ovate, and smooth, and have protruding styles.

Leaves to 1" long, grayish, and densely hairy.

Escaped from cultivation; grows in disturbed areas, vacant lots and fields, and along roads.

Life Zone: Plains

Flowering Time: April to October

Pennycress

(Fanweed, Stinkweed, Frenchweed,
 Mithridate Mustard, Field Cress)

Thlaspi arvense

Mustard Family (Brassicaceae)

Annual, to 2½' tall, with soft,
smooth, twisted stem.

Flowers are small, in ½" clusters
that make up an elongated raceme;
the 4 petals are white. Seed pods
are flat, notched, to ½" long, with
broad margins.

Leaves are alternate; the upper leaves
are stalkless and clasping; lower leaves
are stalked and broader, to 3" long.

Thrives in waste places; common
in fields and along roads.

Life Zones: Plains to Montane

Flowering Time: May to August

Shepherd's Purse

(Shovelweed, Pickpocket)

Capsella bursa-pastoris
(Bursa bursa-pastoris)

Mustard Family (Brassicaceae)

Annual or biennial, to 18" tall, with vertical root and erect, hairy stem.

Flowers are tiny (to ⅛"), with 4 white petals, on stalks and in racemes. Seed pods are triangular and notched at top.

Leaves are mostly basal, deeply toothed or lobed, and woolly. They wilt early.

Common in waste ground, in yards and fields, and along walls and fences.

Life Zones: Plains and Foothills

Flowering Time:
March to December

Watercress

(True Watercress)

Nasturtium officinale
(N. nasturtium-aquaticum,
Rorippa nasturtium-aquaticum,
Radicula nasturtium-aquaticum)

Mustard Family (Brassicaceae)

Perennial, to 18" long, with trailing, creeping, floating, fleshy stems that root at the nodes.

Flowers to ¼" across, with 4 white and reddish petals. The seed pod, to 1" long, is ascending and curved.

Leaves are pinnately divided into ovate, fleshy, smooth leaflets.

Common in shallow water of streams and ponds, on mud banks, and in ditches; European immigrant.

Life Zones: Plains and Foothills

Flowering Time: June to August

Whitetop

(Whiteweed, Hoary Cress, Pepperweed)

Cardaria draba
(Lepidium draba, L. repens)

Mustard Family (Brassicaceae)

Perennial, to 2' tall, in dense patches, with spreading rootstock and stout, hairy, erect or leaning stem.

Flowers are small (¼"), with 4 white petals in flat clusters. Seed pods are tiny, flat, smooth, and 2-lobed.

Leaves are hairy, with pointed tips and toothed margins.

Troublesome weed in fields, yards, vacant lots and waste places, and along roads; Eurasian import.

Life Zones: Plains and Foothills

Flowering Time: April to August

Wild Tomato

(Cut-Leaved Nightshade,
 Three-Flowered Nightshade)

Solanum triflorum

Nightshade Family (Solanaceae)

Annual, to 3' long, with trailing, spreading stem.

Flowers in drooping clusters, with white, 5-lobed corolla. Fruits, to ⅝", are round and green.

Leaves are fleshy and deeply cut into deltoid lobes that are bristly underneath.

Grows in waste places, roadsides, dry fields, and vacant lots.

Life Zones: Plains and Foothills

Flowering Time:
June to September

Wild Onion

(Sand Onion, Textile Onion)

Allium textile

Onion Family (Alliaceae)

Perennial, to 12" high, in clumps, with fibrous bulb and slender, erect stalk.

Flowers are ⅛" wide, in umbel, with 6 white sepals and 6 white petals with red stripes.

Leaves (2) are basal, slender, and grooved.

Grows in dry places, such as deserts, prairie slopes, hillsides, and openings in woods.

Life Zones: Plains and Foothills

Flowering Time: April to June

White Dutch Clover

(White Clover, Dutch Clover)

Trifolium repens

Pea Family (Fabaceae)

Perennial, creeping and rooting at the nodes, to 2' long.

Flowers are white, tannish, or pinkish, in rounded clusters, to 1¼" across.

Leaves are three-parted, on long, slender stalk; leaflets are bright green, to ¾" wide, and sharply toothed.

Grows in moist areas of meadows, lawns, pastures, forest clearings, and roadsides.

Life Zones: Plains to Montane

Flowering Time: April to October

White Prairie Clover

(Prairie Clover, White Petalostemon)

Dalea candida oligophylla
(Petalostemon candidum, P. oligophyllum)

Pea Family (Fabaceae)

Perennial, to 2' tall, with smooth, slender, gland-dotted stems.

Flowers are small (to ¼" long), with 5 clawed, white petals, arranged in dense, cylindrical spikes, to 3" long. Seed pod is tiny (⅛" long), membranous, and enclosed by the calyx.

Leaves are stalked and divided pinnately into 5 to 9, 1" long leaflets.

Common in sandy areas on prairies and mesas, in gullies, and along roads.

Life Zone: Plains

Flowering Time: June to August

White Sweet Clover

Melilotus alba

Pea Family (Fabaceae)

Perennial, to 8' high, in patches, with widely branched, flexible stem.

Flowers are small, white or creamy, fragrant, in long, slender racemes that may contain as many as 80 flowers.

Leaves are palmately compound; the leaflets are about 1" long, with toothed margins.

Escaped from cultivation to roadsides, fields, stream banks, canals, and dams.

Life Zones: Plains to Montane

Flowering Time: May to October

Common Lupine

(Silvery Lupine)

Lupinus argenteus ingratus

Pea Family (Fabaceae)

Perennial, to 3' high, with tough, twisted, hairy stem.

Flowers form narrow, curved racemes, to 6" long. Corolla, ½" long, has spurred, purple keel and white banner. Seed pod is hairy, up to 1" long, and contains 5 seeds.

Leaves are stalked and palmately divided into 2" long, narrow leaflets that are silvery and hairy beneath.

Grows in dry, open spaces in fields and open woods, along roads, and on rocky slopes.

Life Zones: Plains and Foothills

Flowering Time: June to September

Drummond Milkvetch

Astragalus drummondii

Pea Family (Fabaceae)

Perennial, to 2' tall, with stout, leaning, grayish, hairy stems; grows in bunches.

Flowers are creamy white, less than 1" long, in clusters; calyx has scattered black hairs.

Leaves are pinnately compound; the many leaflets are soft, hairy, to ¾" long.

Abundant in dry, open areas, such as hillsides, fields, slopes, and roadsides.

Life Zones: Plains to Montane

Flowering Time: May and June

Standing Milkvetch

(Prairie Milkvetch, Robust Milkvetch,
Shiny Milkvetch, Striate Milkvetch)

Astragalus adsurgens robustior
(A. striatus, A. nitidus)

Pea Family (Fabaceae)

Perennial, to 14" high,
with angular, smooth,
ascending or creeping stems.

Flowers are 2-lipped, in elongate,
dense, long-stalked clusters, with
white, pinkish, or purplish corolla
and black-haired calyx. Pod is ⅜"
long, erect, grooved, and silky.

Leaves are divided into paired, thick,
elliptical leaflets that are silky beneath.

Common on mesas, hillsides, prairies,
and gravelly slopes.

Life Zones: Plains and Foothills

Flowering Time: June and July

Two-Grooved Milkvetch
(Grooved-Pod Vetch)

Astragalus bisulcatus
(Diholcos bisulcatus, Phaca bisulcata)

Pea Family (Fabaceae)

Perennial, to 3' tall, with erect, leafy, shiny stem.

Flowers are whitish, pinkish, or purplish, with ½" long, drooping corolla, and are arranged in long, compact racemes. Seed pods are pointed, slender (⅛" wide), and have 2 prominent grooves.

Leaves comprise 1" long, ovate leaflets (up to 21), hairy beneath.

Common in alkali areas on hillsides and in meadows and parks. *Poisonous:* contains selenium.

Life Zones: Plains and Foothills

Flowering Time: May and June

Scurf Pea
Psoralidium lanceolatum
(Psoralea lanceolata, P. micrantha)

Pea Family (Fabaceae)

Perennial, to 20" tall, with slender, leaning stems that are dotted with resin. Grows in large patches, with long, creeping rootstocks.

Flowers are tiny, in short clusters, with cup-shaped, resin-dotted, hairy calyx and ¼" wide, 2-lipped, white to purplish corolla.

Leaves are stalked and divided into 3 narrow, resin-dotted leaflets.

Grows in dry, sandy areas, such as roadsides, along railroad tracks, on slopes and hillsides, and in waste places.

Life Zones: Plains and Foothills

Flowering Time: May to July

Wild Licorice
Glycyrrhiza lepidota

Pea Family (Fabaceae)

Perennial, to 4' tall, in patches, with thick roots and erect, leafy stems.

Flowers are ½" long, in dense, spike-like raceme with 2-lipped, greenish white corolla. Seed pods are spiny, ½" long burrs.

Leaves are pinnately divided into 1" long, pointed leaflets.

Grows in waste places and along roadsides, railroad tracks, ditches, and streams.

Life Zones:
Plains and Foothills

Flowering Time:
June to August

Spike Gilia
(Spicate Gilia)

Ipomopsis spicata
(Gilia spicata)

Phlox Family (Polemoniaceae)

Perennial, to 12" tall, with taproot and stout, brownish, woolly, erect or curved stem.

Flowers in spikelike, woolly, sticky cluster, with 5 creamy white, reflexed petals.

Leaves are alternate, to 2" long, stringlike, lobed near tip, fleshy, and woolly.

Grows in dry sites on hillsides and slopes, and in open woods.

Life Zones: Plains and Foothills

Flowering Time: April and May

Sticky Gilia

(Pinnate-Leaf Gilia, Alpine Gilia)

Gilia pinnatifida
(G. calcarea)

Phlox Family (Polemoniaceae)

Biennial or perennial, to 20" high, with much-branched, wiry, sticky stem.

Flowers are small (to ⅜" long), with white corolla tube, 5 whitish to lavender lobes, and protruding stamens and pistil.

Leaves are sticky; basal leaves are pinnately divided into ½" long lobes.

Common in open areas in sandy and gravelly soils, among outcrops and rocks, and on slopes, hillsides, and ridges.

Life Zones: Plains to Subalpine

Flowering Time: June to September

Microster

Microsteris gracilis
(M. humilis, M. micrantha)

Phlox Family (Polemoniaceae)

Annual, to 5" tall, with branched, sticky stem.

Flowers are tubular, tiny (to ¼" long), with 5 white petals (tinged with lavender or pink) and 5 bristly sepals.

Leaves are narrowly lanceolate, to 1½" long; the lower leaves are opposite, and the upper ones are alternate.

Very common but often overlooked; grows in open woods and thickets, and on slopes and hillsides.

Life Zones: Plains to Montane

Flowering Time: April to June

Bouncing Bet

(Soapwort)

Saponaria officinalis

Pink Family (Caryophyllaceae)

Perennial, to 3' tall, in dense stands, with erect, sturdy stem.

Flowers are tubular and large (1¼" long), with 5 (sometimes 10) white to pinkish petals.

Leaves are opposite, to 5" long, tapered.

Common in waste places, along roads and streams, near old homesteads, and in fields.

Life Zones: Plains and Foothills

Flowering Time:
June to September

Night-Flowering Catchfly
(Stick Cockle)

Silene noctiflora

Pink Family (Caryophyllaceae)

Annual, to 3' tall, with erect, stiff, sticky, hairy stems.

Flowers are fragrant, with 5 cleft, white to pinkish petals on a long corolla tube, and an ovoid, inflated, green and reddish striped calyx.

Leaves are opposite, to 3 ½" long, sticky, hairy, with elongated tips.

Grows in fallow fields, vacant lots, disturbed areas, and roadsides; Eurasian import.

Life Zones: Plains and Foothills

Flowering Time: May to September

White Campion

(Evening Campion, Evening Lychnis)

Melandrium dioicum
(M. album, Lychnis alba,
L. dioicum, Silene alba)

Pink Family (Caryophyllaceae)

Perennial, to 3' tall, with sturdy, sticky, hairy stem.

Flowers open at night; the five petals are white and deeply notched; calyx is inflated and striped.

Leaves are opposite, to 4" long, hairless, with entire margins.

Common at edges of woods, in thickets, pastures, fields, and along roadsides.

Life Zones: Plains to Montane

Flowering Time: May to September

148

Woolly Plantain

Plantago patagonica

Plantain Family (Plantaginaceae)

Annual, to 8" high, with slender root and wiry, hairy stems.

Flowers are hidden in narrow spikes, to 3" long, and have 4 spreading, white petals and hairy, leaflike bracts.

Leaves are basal, slender, to 4" long, hairy, with parallel veins.

Common in disturbed soil, on overgrazed range, on prairie slopes and hillsides, and along ridges.

Life Zones: Plains and Foothills

Flowering Time: April to June

Prickly Poppy
Argemone polyanthemos

Poppy Family (Papaveraceae)

Annual (maybe perennial), to 4' tall, with orange sap and stout, erect, shiny stem that has scattered prickles.

Flowers are spectacular, 3" across, with 4 to 6 satiny, pure white petals.

Leaves are pale, bluish green, to 8" long, smooth but with spiny veins. Spines are yellow, to ⅜" long, and very sharp.

Abundant in dry, sandy areas along roads, canals, railroad tracks, and on brushy slopes. *Poisonous.*

Life Zones:
Plains and Foothills

Flowering Time:
April to August

Spring Beauty
(Groundnut)
Claytonia rosea
Purslane Family (Portulacaceae)

Perennial, to 6" tall, with round bulb and erect, slender, weak stem.

Flowers are saucer-shaped, to ¾" across, with 5 white to pinkish, red-veined petals.

Leaves are opposite, fleshy, narrowly lance-shaped, with one pair at midstem and (reportedly) 1 or 2 leaves at base. (I haven't seen them; maybe they wither early.)

Common in moist meadows and forest openings, and on shrubby slopes. One of our earliest beauties.

Life Zone: Foothills

Flowering Time: March to May

Bastard Toadflax

(Pale Bastard Toadflax, Pale Comandra,
 Star Toadflax)

Comandra umbellata
(C. pallida)

Sandalwood Family (Santalaceae)

Perennial, to 12" high, in patches,
with woody rootstock and
branched, leafy stems.

Flowers are small (⅛"), without
petals but with white to greenish
or pinkish sepals; flowers are in
dense clusters. Fruit is a ¼" nut.

Leaves are alternate, to 1½" long,
fleshy, bluish green, and pointed.

Common in dry and disturbed areas
in sagebrush, desert, sandy hillsides,
grassy slopes, and open woods.

Life Zones: Plains and Foothills

Flowering Time: April to July

Sidewalk Weed

(Thyme-Leaved Spurge)

Chamaesyce serpyllifolia
(Euphorbia serpyllifolia)

Spurge Family
(Euphorbiaceae)

Annual, with slender taproot and creeping, reddish stems.

Flowers are tiny, white, and segregated by sex; the female flowers have club-shaped styles.

Leaves to ½" long, bluish green, smooth, and ovate, with toothed tips.

Common in sidewalk cracks, along pavement, and in yards, gardens, and disturbed areas.

Life Zone: Plains

Flowering Time: July to October

153

Snow-on-the-Mountain

Agaloma marginata
(Euphorbia marginata,
  Dichrophyllum marginatum)

Spurge Family
(Euphorbiaceae)

Annual, to 3' tall, with milky sap and stout, tough, reddish stem.

Flowers are small, inconspicuous, with white petals and leafy, white-margined bracts, in umbel-like clusters.

Leaves are ovate, to 3½" long; the upper ones are white-margined.

Grows on dry slopes and hillsides.

Life Zone: Plains

Flowering Time: March to October

Wild Poinsettia

Poinsettia dentata
(Euphorbia dentata)

Spurge Family
(Euphorbiaceae)

Annual, to 2' high, with milky sap and much-branched, erect, bright green, hairy, sticky stem.

Flowers are inconspicuous, small, whitish to yellowish green, and grow in clusters. Fruit is ³⁄₁₆" across, smooth, and 3-chambered.

Leaves are opposite, closely spaced, prominently toothed, bright green with reddish spots, pale and hairy beneath, and stalked.

Grows in waste places, fields and yards, and along roads.

Life Zone: Plains

Flowering Time: June to August

155

Giant Evening Star

(Large Evening Star, Ten-Petaled
Blazing Star, Moonflower)

Nuttallia decapetala
(Mentzelia decapetala,
Touteria decapetala)

Stickleaf Family (Loasaceae)

Perennial, to 3' tall, with
erect to reclining stem.

Flowers are large (to 5" across),
spectacular when open in
morning and evening, with
10 white, extended petals
and 100 or so white and silky
stamens.

Leaves are alternate, thick,
with barbed spines and
toothed margins.

Grows in disturbed soil,
on shaley or sandy hillsides,
canyon walls, and prairie
slopes.

Life Zones:
Plains and Foothills

Flowering Time:
July to September

White Evening Star

(Plains Evening Star, Blazing
Star, Stickleaf, Stickweed)

Nuttallia nuda
(Mentzelia nuda,
Touteria nuda)

Stickleaf Family (Loasaceae)

Perennial, to 20" tall, with
white, shiny stems, in clumps.

Flowers are closed during
the day, but spectacular when
open in evenings; the 3" flowers
have 5 creamy white petals
and 5 functional stamens,
plus 50 or so petal-like, non-
functional stamens.

Leaves are thick, pinnately
lobed, to 3" long, rough, with
stiff, barbed hairs.

Grows in dry, sandy areas
along roads, on hillsides,
and in disturbed prairie.

Life Zones:
Plains and Foothills

Flowering Time:
June to August

Scorpion Weed

Phacelia heterophylla
(P. biennis)

Waterleaf Family
(Hydrophyllaceae)

Biennial or perennial, to 2½'
high, with thick, bristly stem.

Flowers are tiny (less than ¼")
and crowded in coiled clusters;
corolla is white at first, then
turns bluish or brownish.

Leaves are alternate, lobed
at base, about 2" long, bristly,
with prominent veins.

Common in disturbed ground,
along roads, and in pastures
and fields.

Life Zones: Plains to Montane

Flowering Time: May to July

Waterleaf

(Fendler Waterleaf, Squaw Lettuce,
 White Cat's Breeches)

Hydrophyllum fendleri

Waterleaf Family (Hydrophyllaceae)

Perennial, to 3' tall, in large patches, with bristly stem.

Flowers are in paired clusters, with 5 white to lavender petals, bristly sepals, and long, protruding stamens.

Leaves to 12" long, divided into 5 to 13 soft, toothed leaflets.

Grows in shade and moist areas, such as stream banks and floodplains, and in woods and thickets.

Life Zones:
Plains to Montane

Flowering Time:
May to July

Rabbitbrush

(False Goldenrod, Goldenbush)

Chrysothamnus nauseosus

Aster Family (Asteraceae)

Shrub, to 5' tall, odorous, bushy, with slender, felty, grayish branches and twigs.

Flower heads are numerous, in dense, rounded clusters, without ray flowers; the 5 disk flowers are ½" long and yellow.

Leaves are linear, pointed, to 3" long, and grayish green.

Abundant in overgrazed and eroded areas, on open slopes, and along roads.

Life Zones: Plains and Foothills

Flowering Time: August to October

Tall Oregon Grape

(Hollygrape, Oregon Grape)

Mahonia aquifolium
(Berberis aquifolium)

Barberry Family (Berberidaceae)

Shrub, to 6' tall, with grayish tan bark that splits vertically and yellow wood.

Flowers are numerous, on short stalks, in yellow clusters. Berries have blue, powdery bloom.

Leaves are evergreen, to 10" long, pinnately divided into 9 or 11 leaflets that are stiff, shiny, and dark green on top, pale beneath, with spiny teeth.

Escapee from cultivation, found along fences and ditches.

Life Zone: Plains

Flowering Time: May and June

Yellow Clematis

(Oriental Clematis)

Viticella orientalis
(Clematis orientalis)

Buttercup Family (Ranunculaceae)

Perennial, woody vine, with slender, wiry, angular stems that can reach 20'. Climbs and covers small trees or shrubs.

Flowers are 2" wide, with long stalks and 4 or 5 dull yellow tepals (undifferentiated petals and sepals) and styles that develop into 2" long, white, silky plumes.

Leaves are opposite, long-stalked, and divided into coarsely toothed, arrow-shaped leaflets.

Found along roads and in thickets; Asian import to mining camps.

Life Zone: Foothills

Flowering Time: July and August

Russian Olive

(Oleaster)

Elaeagnus angustifolia

Oleaster Family (Elaeagnaceae)

Shrub or tree, to 15' tall, with shiny, reddish branches and silvery, spiny twigs.

Flowers are small (¼"), fragrant, with yellow, 4-lobed corolla. The "olives" are oval and silvery, about ¼" wide.

Leaves taper at both ends, to 4" long, silvery and scaly beneath.

Thrives in dry areas; Eurasian escapee from cultivation.

Life Zones: Plains and Foothills

Flowering Time: June

Golden Currant

(Buffalo Currant, Clove Bush)

Ribes aureum
(R. longiflorum, R. longifolium,
R. odovatum)

Gooseberry Family (Grossulariaceae)

Shrub, to 9' tall, with erect or spreading stem and smooth, reddish gray branches.

Flowers are in loose clusters, tubular, with 5 bright yellow, petal-like sepals and short, pale yellow petals. Berries are small (⅜"), round, smooth, and reddish brown to black.

Leaves are divided into 3 to 5 kidney-shaped lobes.

Grows along streams and in ditches and open woods.

Life Zones: Plains and Foothills

Flowering Time: April to June

Three-Leaf Sumac

(Skunkbush, Skunkbrush,
Squawbush, Lemonadebush,
Lemonade Sumac, Polecat Bush)

Rhus aromatica trilobata

Sumac Family (Anacardiaceae)

Shrub, to 6' tall, forming dense thickets, with rank-smelling wood and much-branched stems.

Flowers are tiny (to ⅛"), pale yellow, in tight clusters; flowers appear before leaves. Berries are red, hairy, and sticky.

Leaves are divided into 3, wavy-toothed, 1" long leaflets.

Common in sandy, dry areas, on rocky slopes and canyon sides, and in open woods.

Life Zones:
Plains and Foothills

Flowering Time:
April to June

Wild Asparagus

Asparagus officinalis

Asparagus Family (Asparagaceae)

Perennial, to 6' tall, with branched rootstock and green, much-branched, threadlike branchlets, to ¾" long. Young stems are succulent and edible.

Flowers are small, lilylike, greenish yellow, stalked, and in pairs.

Leaves are small, scalelike, and inconspicuous.

Grows in fields and along roads and irrigation ditches; Mediterranean escapee.

Life Zone: Plains

Flowering Time: May and June

Arrowleaf Balsamroot

(Balsamroot, Big Sunflower, Bigroot)

Balsamorhiza sagittata

Aster Family (Asteraceae)

Perennial, to 2' tall, occurs in large masses, with many woody, hairy stems and a stout taproot.

Flower heads are single, large (to 4" across), with many yellow, tubular disk-flowers, woolly bracts, and to 25 bright yellow ray flowers.

Leaves are arrow-shaped, mostly basal, to 12" long (including stalks), and densely hairy beneath (whitish).

Common in western Colorado; on sunny hillsides, in grassy flats, in open woods, and on sagebrush slopes.

Life Zones: Plains to Montane

Flowering Time: April to August

Beggar's Tick

(Bur Marigold, Sticktight)

Bidens frondosa

Aster Family (Asteraceae)

Annual, to 3' tall, with reddish, opposite branches.

Flower heads have no ray flowers; the disk flowers are ⅜" long, 5-toothed, dark yellow to orange, and enclosed by 1" long bracts.

Leaves are opposite and either simple or dissected into 3 leaflets that have many teeth.

Grows in moist areas, such as swamps, bogs, pond shores, ditches, and waste places.

Life Zones: Plains and Foothills

Flowering Time: July to October

168

Broom Senecio

(Grassleaf Senecio)

Senecio spartioides

Aster Family (Asteraceae)

Perennial, to 30" tall, in large clumps, with erect, leafy stems.

Flower heads are numerous, about 1½" across, with small, dark yellow disks, narrow, pale yellow ray flowers (fewer than 10), and pointed bracts, to ⅜" long.

Leaves are alternate, to 3½" long, slender, and lobed at the base.

Grows in disturbed soils along roads, on burrowed hillsides, and at the edges of woods.

Life Zones:
Plains to Montane

Flowering Time:
July to September

Colorado Greenthread

(Rayless Greenthread)

Thelesperma megapotamicum
(T. gracile)

Aster Family (Asteraceae)

Perennial, to 3' tall, with erect, wiry, hairless, grooved stem.

Flower heads are cup-shaped, ½" high, on long stalks, with no ray flowers. The disk flowers are golden yellow to orange and surrounded by 3 layers of bracts; the inner bracts are papery, the middle ones fused and pointed, and the outer ones fleshy and recurved.

Leaves are opposite, to 4" long, and pinnately divided into threadlike segments.

Grows in dry areas, along roads, and on rocky hillsides and mesas.

Life Zone: Plains

Flowering Time: May to October

Common Sow Thistle

(Milk Thistle, Annual Sow Thistle)

Sonchus oleraceus

Aster Family (Asteraceae)

Annual, to 3' tall, with leafy, reddish, grooved stem.

Flower heads are small, in loose clusters, with pale yellow ray flowers and slender bracts with tannish margins. The one-seeded fruit is ribbed and wrinkled.

Leaves are deeply lobed, with spiny teeth; the upper lobe is large and arrowhead-shaped.

Common in fields, roadsides, waste places, and cultivated ground; European immigrant.

Life Zone: Plains

Flowering Time: June to October

Cream Tips

(Woolly-White, Woolly Hymenopappus)

Hymenopappus filifolius cinereus
(H. cinereus, H. polycephalus)

Aster Family (Asteraceae)

Perennial, to 2' tall, branched into several wiry, whitish stems.

Flower heads are small, on long stalks, with no ray flowers but about 20, pale yellow disk flowers and green and white, woolly bracts.

Leaves are bunched and dissected into linear, fleshy, hairy segments.

Common in dry, exposed areas on grassy slopes and hillsides.

Life Zones: Plains and Foothills

Flowering Time: May to September

Common Dandelion

(Dandelion, Blowball)

Taraxacum officinale

Aster Family (Asteraceae)

Perennial, to 18" tall; hollow, leafless flower stalks contain a milky juice.

Flower heads to 2" wide, without disk flowers. Ray flowers are golden yellow; the inner ones are erect, and the outer ones are spreading. Inner bracts are long and erect; the outer ones are broad and curl back.

Leaves, forming basal rosette, are up to 12" long, hairless, and coarsely toothed.

Found almost everywhere, in pastures, roadsides, thickets, open woods, and lawns.

Life Zones:
Plains to Alpine

Flowering Time:
March to November

Wavyleaf Dandelion

(Longleaf Dandelion, False Dandelion)

Nothocalais cuspidata
(Agoseris cuspidata, Microseris cuspidata, Troximon cuspidata)

Aster Family (Asteraceae)

Perennial, to 10" tall, with leafless, woolly stems.

Flower heads are 2" across, without disk flowers; the ray flowers are bright yellow (reddish on back), and the bracts are long, pointed, green, purple, and white.

Leaves are basal, to 6" long, fleshy, and soft, with wavy, hairy margins.

Common early flower in dry, open prairie and on gravelly hillsides, rocky slopes, and mesas.

Life Zones: Plains and Foothills

Flowering Time: April to June

Golden Aster
Heterotheca horrida
Aster Family (Asteraceae)

Perennial, to 9" tall, in bunches, with woody, purplish, sticky stems that branch near the top.

Flower heads to ¾" across, on slender, sticky stalks, with yellow ray flowers, orange disks, and tiered, sticky bracts.

Leaves on stem are grayish green, stalkless, sticky, leathery, and spatula-shaped; lower leaves are stalked, to 1" long, and wither early.

Grows in dry areas on slopes and hillsides, in fields and open woods, and along roads.

Life Zones: Foothills and Montane

Flowering Time: July to September

Goldeneye

(Golden Aster)

Heterotheca canescens
(Chrysopsis canescens, C. arida,
C. bakeri, C. villosa)

Aster Family (Asteraceae)

Perennial, to 20" tall, in clumps, with erect, leaning, grayish, hairy stems.

Flower heads to 1" across, clustered, with tan or orange disks; ray flowers are golden yellow, narrow, and many; bracts are hairy, with dark tips and whitish margins.

Leaves to 2" long, thick, leathery, twisted, and hairy.

Common in dry, sunny areas, especially roadsides but also in deserts and fields, and on hillsides and rocky slopes.

Life Zones: Plains to Montane

Flowering Time: July to October

Common Goldenrod

(Meadow Goldenrod, Canada Goldenrod,
 Tall Goldenrod)

Solidago canadensis

Aster Family (Asteraceae)

Perennial, to 5' tall, with erect, leafy, hairy stems.

Flower heads are bell-shaped, ¼" high, in long, one-sided racemes, with few golden yellow ray flowers, dark yellow disk flowers, and green and white bracts.

Leaves to 5" long, leathery, with toothed margins; leaves hug the stem.

Grows in moist areas, such as meadows, open woods, and stream banks.

Life Zones: Plains to Montane

Flowering Time: July to September

177

Few-Flowered Goldenrod

Solidago sparsiflora
(S. trinervata, S. velutina)

Aster Family (Asteraceae)

Perennial, in patches, to 2' tall, with leaning, wiry, hairy stems.

Flower heads are small (to ⅜" high), in one-sided racemes; ray flowers are few or absent, and the few disk flowers are yellow to coppery and 5-lobed. Bracts are slender, green and white, in 4 tiers.

Stem leaves are much smaller than basal leaves, which are stalked, to 4" long, spatulate, and bristly on the margins, and wither early.

Grows on hillsides and road cuts, and in pastures and fields.

Life Zones: Plains to Montane

Flowering Time: July to September

Late Goldenrod
(Tall Goldenrod)

Solidago serotinoides
(S. gigantea, S. pitcheri, S. serotina)

Aster Family (Asteraceae)

Perennial, to 7' tall, in clumps, with stout, smooth, leafy stem.

Flower heads are many, small, bell-shaped, golden yellow, in long, one-sided racemes, with linear, whitish, tiered bracts.

Leaves are narrowly lance-shaped, to 5" long, sharp-tipped, and toothed.

Grows in moist sites along canals and streams.

Life Zones: Plains and Foothills

Flowering Time: July to September

Rough Goldenrod

(Low Goldenrod)

Solidago nana
(S. pulcherrima, S. radulina)

Aster Family (Asteraceae)

Perennial, in tufts, to 32" tall, with branched, leafy, hairy, curved stems.

Flower heads are crowded in a pyramid-shaped panicle; bracts are tiered, slender, pointed, and green and white.

Leaves are rough, hairy, to 2" long, spatulate, with pointed tips.

Grows in dry areas, such as waste ground, roadsides, edges of thickets, and sandy slopes.

Life Zones: Plains to Montane

Flowering Time: July to September

Tall Goldenrod

Solidago altissima
(S. polyphylla)

Aster Family (Asteraceae)

Perennial, to 6' tall, in tufts, with erect, hairy stems.

Flower heads are smaller than ¼", in large (to 12" long), one-sided clusters, with a few golden yellow ray flowers, yellow disks, and slender, green and white bracts.

Leaves to 6" long, sharply toothed, prominently 3-veined, and soft and hairy beneath.

Grows in moist habitats along roads, ditches, and streams, and in meadows, open woods, and thickets.

Life Zones: Plains to Montane

Flowering Time: August to November

Western Goldenrod

Euthamia occidentalis
(Solidago occidentalis)

Aster Family (Asteraceae)

Perennial, to 6' tall, with slender, bright green, hairless, ribbed stem.

Flower heads are small (to ¼") and have bright yellow ray flowers and disk flowers. Flower heads form small clusters that make up a loose, flat-topped cluster.

Leaves are bright green, narrow, to 4" long, clasping, with 3 veins, bristly margins, and resin dots.

Grows in moist places in valleys.

Life Zones:
Plains and Foothills

Flowering Time:
July to October

Golden Tickseed

(Painted Daisy, Golden Wave,
 Plains Coreopsis)

Coreopsis tinctoria
(C. cardaminifolia)

Aster Family
(Asteraceae)

Annual, to 3' tall, in
bunches, with erect,
smooth, slender stems.

Flower heads to 2" across,
with bright yellow ray flowers,
dark brown disks, and reddish
brown inner bracts.

Leaves are mostly basal and
pinnately divided into linear
segments.

Found on mud flats, pond
shores, fields, and waste places
east of the Continental Divide.

Life Zone: Plains

Flowering Time: June to August

Goldweed

(Cowpen Daisy, Crownbeard)

Ximenesia encelioides
(Verbesina encelioides)

Aster Family (Asteraceae)

Annual, to 2' tall, smelly, with much-branched, hairy, grayish stem.

Flower heads are 1" across, on long stalks, with golden yellow to orange ray flowers, orange disks, and bristly bracts.

Leaves are coarsely toothed, whitish, and densely hairy underneath.

Common in corrals, vacant lots, waste places, and pastures.

Life Zone: Plains

Flowering Time:
June to October

Green Eyes

(Chocolate Flower, Chocolate Daisy,
Green-Eyed Lyre Leaf)

Berlandiera lyrata

Aster Family (Asteraceae)

Perennial, to 4' tall, with fleshy taproot and leafy, erect stem.

Flower heads to 1 ½" wide, with bright yellow, red-veined ray flowers that smell like chocolate, maroon disks, and large, petal-like bracts.

Leaves are pinnately lobed, toothed, whitish, and hairy beneath.

Grows in dry places in southeastern Colorado, along roads and on alkali flats and limy, grassy slopes.

Life Zone: Plains

Flowering Time: April to October

Gumweed

(Resinweed, Tarweed,
 Gumplant, Curly Cup)

Grindelia squarrosa

Aster Family (Asteraceae)

Perennial, to 3'
tall, with tough, wiry,
reddish stem.

Flower heads to 1½",
sticky, aromatic, with
many yellow ray flowers,
small, yellow disk, and
sticky, curled bracts.

Leaves are stalkless, stiff,
and toothed.

Abundant in waste places,
abandoned fields, and
along roads.

Life Zones:
Plains and Foothills

Flowering Time:
July to October

Perennial Bahia

Picradeniopsis oppositifolia
(Bahia oppositifolia)

Aster Family (Asteraceae)

Perennial, to 10" high, with woody, much-branched, gray, hairy stem.

Flower heads are small, with only a few ray flowers and 20 or more disk flowers (both yellow) clustered at top on short, hairy stalks. Bracts are leaflike, gray, hairy, and keeled.

Leaves are mostly opposite and dissected into 3 to 5 linear, gray, hairy, fleshy lobes.

Grows on dry hillsides and along roads.

Life Zones: Plains and Foothills

Flowering Time: June to September

Perky Sue

(Stemless Hymenoxys, Actinea)

Tetraneuris acaulis
(Hymenoxys acaulis, Actinea acaulis)

Aster Family (Asteraceae)

Perennial, to 16" high, with rootstock. The plant is stemless or has a short stem above the ground, but the flower stalks can be mistaken for stems.

Flower heads are large (to 1½" across), on long, silvery, woolly stalks that can be a mere 2" high when flowering starts. The ray flowers are lemon yellow with orange veins; disk flowers are yellow and waxy; bracts are ovate, hairy, and whitish.

Leaves are silky, narrow, fleshy, and dotted.

Grows in dry, rocky places on hillsides and mesas.

Life Zones: Plains and Foothills

Flowering Time: May to September

Pineapple Weed

(Wild Chamomile)

Lepidotheca suaveolens
(Chamomilla suaveolens, Matricaria
suaveolens, M. matricarioides)

Aster Family (Asteraceae)

Annual, to 20" tall, with erect
or sprawling stems that are fleshy,
much-branched, and hairless.
Smells like pineapple.

Flower heads are dome- or cone-
shaped, without ray flowers; the
disk flowers are greenish yellow,
and the bracts are very short (⅛"),
oval, with papery margins.

Leaves are dissected 3 times into
short, threadlike lobes.

Common in disturbed areas, such
as roadsides, abandoned fields,
trailheads, and picnic areas.

Life Zones: Foothills and Montane

Flowering Time: June to October

Plains Zinnia

(Prairie Zinnia, Wild Zinnia, Rocky
  Mountain Zinnia, Little Golden Zinnia,
  Golden Paper Flower)

Zinnia grandiflora
(Crassina grandiflora)

Aster Family (Asteraceae)

Perennial, to 8" high, in clumps,
with woody, leafy stems.

Flower heads resemble buttercups,
with dark red disk flowers and broad
petal-like ray flowers that are yellow
and papery when old.

Leaves are opposite, narrow, to
1½" long.

Found in southeastern Colorado
in dry, limy soils, in deserts and on
rocky hillsides and gravelly slopes.

Life Zone: Plains

Flowering Time: June to October

190

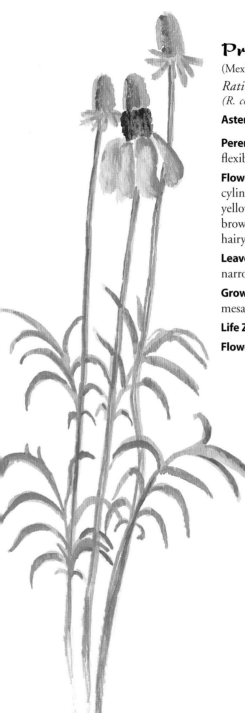

Prairie Coneflowers

(Mexican Hat)

Ratibida columnifera
(R. columnaris, Lepachys columnaris)

Aster Family (Asteraceae)

Perennial, to 2½' tall, with leafy, flexible, slender stems.

Flower heads are cone-shaped, cylindrical, to 2½" high, with golden yellow, drooping ray flowers, dark brown to purple disk flowers, and hairy, grayish, leaflike bracts.

Leaves are pinnately dissected into narrow, hairy lobes.

Grows in limy soil along roads and on mesas, prairie slopes, and hillsides.

Life Zones: Plains and Foothills

Flowering Time: June to September

Prairie Sage

(White Sage, Western Ragwort,
Western Mugwort)

Artemisia ludoviciana
(A. brittonii, A. diversifolia, A. gnaphalodes,
A. pabularis, A. pudica, A. purshiana,
A. silvicola)

Aster Family (Asteraceae)

Perennial, to 3' tall, with slender root-stock and silvery, velvety, erect stems.

Flower heads are tiny (³⁄₁₆"), in spikelike panicle, with whitish, woolly bracts and yellow flowers.

Leaves vary from entire to deeply lobed; leaves are white, woolly beneath, to 3" long.

Common in dry areas on prairie slopes and gravelly hillsides, along roads and railroad tracks, and in waste ground and open woods.

Life Zones: Plains to Montane

Flowering Time: July to October

Prickly Lettuce

(Compass Plant)

Lactuca serriola
(L. scariola)

Aster Family (Asteraceae)

Annual, to 4' tall, with milky sap and much-branched stem.

Flower heads are numerous, ½" high, with pale yellow, toothed ray flowers and slender, green bracts.

Leaves are deeply lobed and erect, with spiny midribs and margins; the upper leaves are small and entire.

Found in dry soil, along ditches and roadsides, and in fields and gardens.

Life Zone: Plains

Flowering Time: July to October

Ragwort

(Groundsel, Old Man)

Packera plattensis
(Senecio plattensis, S. balsamitae,
* S. mutabilis)*

Aster Family (Asteraceae)

Perennial, in clumps, to 20" tall, with stout, cobwebby stems.

Flower heads are ¾" wide, on long stalks, forming umbel-like clusters. Ray flowers are golden yellow; the disk is yellow to orange and domed; bracts are narrow, light green, and velvety.

Leaves are fleshy, woolly, toothed, and lyre-shaped.

Grows in dry areas in eastern Colorado, on prairies, bluffs, mesas, and grassy slopes.

Life Zones: Plains and Foothills

Flowering Time: May to August

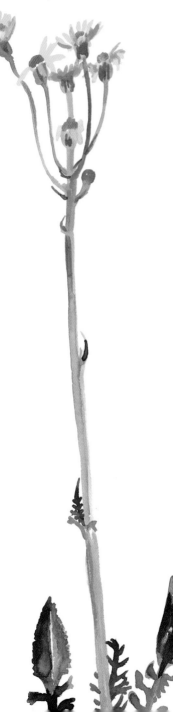

False Salsify

Podospermum laciniatum
(Scorzonera laciniata)

Aster Family (Asteraceae)

Perennial, to 20" tall, with smooth, hollow, grooved, flexible stem.

Flower heads are on long stalks, with dull yellow, orange-tipped ray flowers, bright yellow disk, and 1" long, keeled, pointed, green and brown bracts.

Leaves to 4" long, velvety, and pinnately dissected into slender, pointed lobes.

Common in disturbed soil along roads and in grassy areas.

Life Zone: Plains

Flowering Time: April to July

Meadow Salsify

(Oyster Plant, Goat's Beard)

Tragopogon pratensis

Aster Family (Asteraceae)

Biennial, to 2' tall, with fleshy taproot and milky juice; stems are hollow, erect but curved, smooth, and light green.

Flower head is single, large (to 2" across), closed in sunlight; ray flowers (up to 20) are dull yellow, with toothed tips; bracts are shorter than ray flowers, light green with purple margins, and sharp-tipped. Seed heads to 3½" across, round, white and tawny-colored.

Leaves are narrow, clasping, curled, and toothed.

Found in waste places, roadsides, pastures, and fields.

Life Zones: Plains to Montane

Flowering Time: June to August

Yellow Salsify

(Goat's Beard)

Tragopogon dubius major

Aster Family (Asteraceae)

Perennial, to 4' tall, with milky sap and erect, hollow stem, swollen at top.

Flower head is large (to 2" across), without disk flowers. The outer ray flowers are long and pale yellow; the inner ones are short, with brown styles. Seed heads are large (to 4" across) with brownish seeds tufted with silky bristles. Bracts are long (to 3"), slender, pointed, and extend beyond ray flowers.

Leaves are narrow, to 12" long, grasslike.

Found in waste places, such as roadsides, vacant lots, and fields; European immigrant.

Life Zones: Plains and Foothills

Flowering Time: May to August

Snakeweed

(Broomweed, Broom Snakeweed,
 Gold Top, Matchbush, Turpentine Weed)

*Gutierrezia sarothrae
(G. diversifolia)*

Aster Family (Asteraceae)

Perennial, to 30" high, bushy,
with many woody, leafy stems.

Flower heads to ¼", crowded
into clusters. Ray flowers are
female, and disk flowers are
male; both are yellow. Bracts
are green-tipped, with papery
margins.

Leaves are threadlike, to
2½" long.

Very common on eroding slopes,
but also grows in other sunny,
dry areas, such as deserts, hillsides,
fields, and roadsides.

Life Zones: Plains to Montane

Flowering Time:
August and September

Common Sunflower

(Kansas Sunflower, Mirasol)

Helianthus annuus
(H. aridus, H. lenticularis)

Aster Family (Asteraceae)

Annual, to 10' tall, with rough, stout, hairy, red-splotched stem.

Flower heads are large (to 5" across), tilted toward the sun, with bright yellow ray flowers, brown to black disks, and broad, bristly, pointed bracts.

Leaves are large (to 10" long), rough, hairy, long-stalked, with toothed margins.

Common along roadsides, on open hillsides and prairie slopes, and in fields and vacant lots.

Life Zones: Plains and Foothills

Flowering Time:
June to September

Little Sunflower

(Aspen Sunflower)

Helianthella uniflora
(H. multicaulis)

Aster Family (Asteraceae)

Perennial, to 3' tall, with bristly, branched stems.

Flower heads are large (to 2½" wide), with brownish, purplish, or yellow disks, bright yellow ray flowers, and spiny, hairy bracts.

Leaves to 8" long, stalked, lance-shaped, bristly on both sides.

Common in aspen groves and clearings in woods and forests, along trails and roads, and on slopes.

Life Zones: Plains to Subalpine

Flowering Time: June to August

Prairie Sunflower

(Narrowleaf Sunflower)

Helianthus petiolaris

Aster Family
(Asteraceae)

Annual, to 3' tall, with erect, reddish, hairy to bristly stems.

Flower heads to 3" across, with bright yellow ray flowers, purplish brown disks, and whitish, hairy bracts.

Leaves are alternate and rough, with long stalks.

Common in waste areas and fields, along roads, and on hillsides.

Life Zones:
Plains and Foothills

Flowering Time:
June to September

Tall Marsh Sunflower

(Tuberous Sunflower, Nuttall Sunflower)

Helianthus nuttallii
(H. fascicularis)

Aster Family (Asteraceae)

Perennial, to 10' tall, with tuberous roots and slender, leafy, reddish stems.

Flower heads are numerous, to 2½" across, with 15 or more bright yellow ray flowers, small, yellow or brownish disks, and slender, pointed, bristly bracts.

Leaves are narrow, to 6" long; the upper leaves are alternate, with entire margins, and the lower leaves are opposite, with toothed margins.

Common on wet sites, such as marshes, sloughs, irrigation ditches, stream banks, and meadows.

Life Zones: Plains and Foothills

Flowering Time: July to September

202

Threadleaf Yellowrays

(Greenthread, Golden Wave,
False Golden Wave, Field Coreopsis)

Thelesperma filifolium
(T. trifidum, T. tenue)

Aster Family (Asteraceae)

Annual or perennial, to 2' tall,
with taproot and smooth, slender,
bright green stems.

Flower heads to 2" wide, drooping,
with 8 bright yellow, broad ray flowers
and yellow to reddish brown disks.
Flowers have broad, fused inner bracts
and 8 linear, outer bracts.

Leaves are divided into weak, threadlike, 1" long segments.

Found in dry, open areas of eastern
Colorado, on prairie slopes, mesas,
and hillsides.

Life Zones: Plains and Foothills

Flowering Time: May to July

Western Hawksbeard

Psilochenia occidentalis
(Crepis occidentalis)

Aster Family (Asteraceae)

Perennial, to 16" tall, with stout, erect, sticky, hairy stems.

Flower heads are in clusters, without disk flowers; the ray flowers are bright yellow, and the bracts are sticky, hairy, and dark gray.

Leaves are thick, pinnately lobed, grayish, hairy, and sticky.

Common in dry, exposed areas on mesas, grassy slopes, and hillsides.

Life Zones: Plains and Foothills

Flowering Time: May to August

Narrowleaf Puccoon

(Fringed Puccoon,
 Fringed Gromwell)

Lithospermum incisum

Borage Family
(Boraginaceae)

Perennial, to 20" high, in circular clumps, with leafy, bristly stems.

Flowers are trumpet-shaped, to 1½" long; the 5 flaring lobes are bright yellow and fringed. Fruits are 4 hard, shiny nuts, about ⅛" long.

Leaves are alternate, firm, to 2½" long.

Common in dry areas on hillsides, gravelly slopes, mesas, and prairies, and in meadows and openings in woods.

Life Zones: Plains to Montane

Flowering Time: April to July

Brittle Cactus

(Fragile Prickly Pear, Potato Cactus)

Opuntia fragilis

Cactus Family (Cactaceae)

Perennial, with 3" wide, potato-like branches (joints) that break off easily. Spines are 1" long and whitish.

Flowers are large (to 2" across), yellowish to greenish, or even pinkish; flowers do not bloom every year. The fruit is oval, tan, ½" long.

Grows on sunny slopes and hillsides, dry prairies, deserts, mesas, and in rocky, open woods.

Life Zones: Plains and Foothills

Flowering Time: May and June

Prickly Pear Cactus

(Bigroot Cactus)

Opuntia macrorhiza
(O. compressa)

Cactus Family (Cactaceae)

Perennial, with woody root and large, ovate pads (to 8" long) that have clusters of spines and bristles about 1" apart. Spines are white, with dark bases, to 2" long.

Flowers are spectacular, to 3" across, with yellow petals (sometimes tinged reddish) and large, green pistil. Fruit is club-shaped, 2" long, fleshy, and dark red.

Common in eastern Colorado on mesas, ridges, desert flats, and rocky slopes.

Life Zone: Plains

Flowering Time: May and June

Hen-and-Chickens

(Greenball Cactus, Green-Flowered
 Hedgehog Cactus)

Echinocereus viridiflorus

Cactus Family (Cactaceae)

Perennial, to 3" high, spherical
to cylindrical, without branches
(joints), but with vertical ridges
that have white, ½" long spines.

Flowers are greenish yellow
(brownish outside) and encircle
the plant.

Common in deserts and open
woods, and on dry prairie
slopes and grassy hillsides.

Life Zones: Plains and Foothills

Flowering Time: May to July

Puncture Vine

(Goat's Head, Caltrop, Bur Nut)

Tribulus terrestris

Caltrop Family (Zygophyllaceae)

Annual, with creeping, much-branched, slender, hairy stems.

Flowers are small, with 5 pale yellow petals and 5 pointed, green and white sepals. Fruit is hard, crested, and splits into 5 spiny segments, the "goats' heads."

Leaves are pinnately divided into 5 to 7 pairs of leaflets.

Common in sandy areas along roads and in abandoned fields, vacant lots, sidewalks, and yards; Mediterranean escapee.

Life Zone: Plains

Flowering Time: April to October

Musineon

Musineon divaricatum
(M. pedunculatum)

Celery Family (Apiaceae)

Perennial, to 12" high, with thick, fleshy taproot, erect, curving stems, and forklike branches.

Flowers are small, with 5 yellow petals, in clusters that form 1" umbels.

Leaves, forming basal rosette, are long-stalked, sheathed at base, and pinnately divided into lobed leaflets.

Abundant in eastern Colorado, on mesas, hillsides, and prairie slopes.

Life Zone: Plains

Flowering Time: April and May

Common Evening Primrose

(Yellow Evening Primrose, Showy
 Evening Primrose, Erect Evening
 Primrose, Hooker's Evening Primrose)

Oenothera villosa
(O. strigosa, O. hookeri, O. rydbergia)

Evening Primrose Family
(Onagraceae)

Biennial, to 4' tall, with erect,
unbranched, woolly stem.

Flowers are tubular (1½" long),
with 4 bright yellow or orange
petals that close during the day,
and 4 leaf-like, turned-down sepals.

Leaves are alternate, grayish, and
woolly, with sharp tips and short
teeth.

Common in open areas, waste places,
and disturbed soil along roadsides,
fences, and irrigation ditches.

Life Zones: Plains and Foothills

Flowering Time: July to September

Golden Evening Primrose

(Yellow Evening Primrose)

Oenothera flava
(Lavauxia flava)

Evening Primrose Family (Onagraceae)

Perennial, with fleshy, thick taproot and no stem.

Flowers are 1½" across, with 4 golden yellow petals that turn reddish in bright sunlight; the fruit is oval, fleshy, to 1½" long, and striped.

Leaves are in a basal rosette, narrow, to 8" long, with large teeth.

Found in dry, exposed areas, such as rocky slopes, roadsides, ridges, and meadows.

Life Zones: Plains to Montane

Flowering Time: May to August

Yellow Stemless Evening Primrose

(Golden Evening Primrose)

Oenothera howardii
*(O. brachycarpa, Lavauxia
brachycarpa)*

Evening Primrose Family
(Onagraceae)

Perennial, to 16" high, spreading, with short, fleshy, light green and reddish stem.

Flowers are large, with 4 broad, bright yellow to reddish petals and 4 yellowish green sepals on long (to 6") stalklike tubes.

Leaves are large, stalked, tapering at both ends, soft, and bluish green.

Grows along roads and on dry slopes, shale banks, and hillsides.

Life Zones: Plains and Foothills

Flowering Time: May to July

Butter-and-Eggs

(Toadflax)

Linaria vulgaris

Figwort Family (Scrophulariaceae)

Perennial, to 3' tall, in dense patches, with slender, erect, unbranched, leafy stems.

Flowers are 2-lipped, spurred, to 1" long, yellow and orange, in dense racemes.

Leaves are entire, to 4" long, grayish green, and ascending.

Common in disturbed areas, such as roadsides, trails, campgrounds, and around mines.

Life Zones: Plains to Montane

Flowering Time: June to October

Tall Butter-and-Eggs

(Dalmatian Toadflax, Toadflax)

Linaria genistifolia dalmatica

Figwort Family (Scrophulariaceae)

Perennial, to 4' tall, in patches, with robust, smooth, powdery, erect stems.

Flowers are arranged in an elongate cluster (to 6" long); the 2-lipped, yellow and orange corolla has a 1" spur on its lower lip.

Leaves are oval, alternate, to 3" long, clasping, soft, and bluish green.

Found along roads and on hillsides, open slopes, and sagebrush flats; European import.

Life Zones: Plains and Foothills

Flowering Time: July and August

Common Mullein

(Mullein, Great Mullein, Woolly Mullein, Flannel Plant)

Verbascum thapsus

Figwort Family (Scrophulariaceae)

Biennial, to 6' tall, with coarse, woolly, partially woody stem.

Flowers are in long (to 2'), dense spike, with 5 bright yellow petals and a 5-lobed, woolly calyx.

Leaves are large (to 16" long), soft, woolly, yellowish or grayish green; the upper leaves are much smaller than lower leaves.

Grows on roadsides, disturbed areas, overgrazed pastures, and fallow fields; European immigrant.

Life Zones: Plains and Foothills

Flowering Time: June to September

Yellow Owlclover

(Gold Tongue)

Orthocarpus luteus

Figwort Family (Scrophulariaceae)

Annual, to 20" tall, with flexible, erect, sticky, hairy stem that branches like a candelabra.

Flowers are golden yellow, with two lips hidden by leaflike bracts, on spikes to 5" long. Seed pods are beanlike.

Leaves are alternate, 3-lobed, stalkless, to 1½" long.

Common in exposed areas, such as prairies, meadows, pastures, fields, and open woods.

Life Zones: Plains to Montane

Flowering Time: June to September

Golden Smoke

(Scrambled Eggs, Curvepod,
 Golden Fumeroot)

Corydalis aurea

Fumitory Family (Fumariaceae)

Biennial, to 16" high, in clumps,
with slender, erect to prostrate stems.

Flowers are yellow, in long clusters,
with one petal expanded into a sac-
like spur.

Leaves are twice-dissected into
wedge-shaped lobes that are soft
and bluish green.

Common in disturbed areas, along
roads and streams, on sandy slopes,
and in open woods.

Life Zones: Plains to Montane

Flowering Time:
February to September

Yellow Columbine

(Golden Columbine)

Aquilegia chrysantha rydbergii

Hellebore Family (Helleboraceae)

Perennial, to 4' tall, bushy.

Flowers are large (to 3½" long). The 5 yellow, scoop-shaped petals have long spurs, and the 5 bright yellow sepals are spreading and pointed; the many stamens and 5 pistils are long and protruding.

Leaves are divided into deeply cleft lobes that are rounded and up to 1½" across.

Grows in moist and sheltered areas in southern Colorado.

Life Zones: Foothills and Montane

Flowering Time: July and August

219

False Flax

Camelina microcarpa

Mustard Family (Brassicaceae)

Annual, to 28" tall, with erect, slender, twisted stem.

Flowers are small (⅛"), with 4 light yellow petals and 4 reddish green sepals.

Leaves are fleshy, with bristly margins; the stem leaves are clasping, and the lower leaves are stalked and slightly toothed.

Common along roads and in waste places and fallow fields.

Life Zones: Plains and Foothills

Flowering Time: April to July

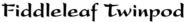

Fiddleleaf Twinpod

(Double Bladderpod)

Physaria vitulifera

Mustard Family (Brassicaceae)

Perennial, to 8" tall, with many curved, sticky, grayish stems.

Flowers grow in clusters; the 4 petals are spatulate and bright yellow, and the 4 sepals are pale green and hairy; the 6 stamens and long style protrude. Seed pods are divided vertically.

Leaves are grayish green and hairy; the stem leaves are small, but the basal leaves are up to 2½" long and fiddle-shaped.

Common in dry areas, such as gravelly slopes and sandy hillsides, and in valleys and canyons.

Life Zones: Plains to Montane

Flowering Time: May to July

Golden Prince's Plume

(Bushy Prince's Plume, Desert Plume,
 Prince's Plume)

Stanleya pinnata
(S. arcuata, S. canescens, S. glauca)

Mustard Family (Brassicaceae)

Perennial, to 5' tall, with stout, erect,
leafy stems that have woody bases.

Flowers are in spikelike racemes
(to 12" long), with 4 yellow, linear,
⅝" long sepals. Seed pods are slender,
to 2½" long, curved, and twisted.

Leaves are lobed, to 6" long.

Grows in dry areas, such as deserts,
prairie slopes, and gravelly hillsides.
Poisonous — absorbs selenium.

Life Zones: Plains and Foothills

Flowering Time: May to July

Mountain Bladderpod

(Bladderpod)

Lesquerella montana
(L. curvipes)

Mustard Family (Brassicaceae)

Perennial, to 8" high, with many slender, hairy stems radiating from one root.

Flowers are pale yellow, ⅜" across, in clusters, with 4 petals on S-curved stalks. The fruit is oblong, to 5⁄16" long, hairy, and bladderlike.

Leaves are mostly basal, stalked, hairy and gray beneath, to 1½" long, and entire or toothed.

Common on dry, sandy hillsides and along roads.

Life Zones: Plains to Montane

Flowering Time: May and June

Tansy Mustard

Descurainia sophia

Mustard Family (Brassicaceae)

Annual, to 30" tall, with stout, curved stem.

Flowers are in crowded clusters; the 4 petals are pale yellow, and the 4 sepals are bright green. Seed pods are linear and 1¼" long.

Leaves to 4" long and divided into threadlike lobes that are bright green and velvety.

Found on disturbed ground, neglected fields, pastures, and roadsides.

Life Zones: Plains to Montane

Flowering Time: April to August

Tumble Mustard

(Jim Hill Mustard)

Sisymbrium altissimum
(Norta altissima)

Mustard Family (Brassicaceae)

Annual, to 4' tall, bushy, with stout, smooth, pithy stem.

Flowers are numerous, form small clusters, and have 4 pale yellow petals. Seed pods are slender, to 4" long, rigid, and spreading.

Leaves are pinnately cleft: the upper leaves into linear segments, and the lower leaves into broader, lobed leaflets that wither early.

Common in vacant lots and along ditches, roads, and railroad tracks. Jim Hill was a railroad magnate.

Life Zones: Plains and Foothills

Flowering Time: April to August

Western Wallflower

(Plains Wallflower, Blister Cress)

Erysimum asperum
(E. aridum, E. elatum,
  E. bakeri, E. asperrimum,
  E. argillosum, E. oblanceolatum)

Mustard Family (Brassicaceae)

Biennial, to 30" tall, with erect, stout stem.

Flowers are grouped in terminal clusters, with ½" long, golden yellow petals. Seed pods are angular, to 4" long.

Leaves are linear, to 4" long, with short teeth.

Grows in open areas, such as slopes, mountain meadows, and open woods.

Life Zones:
Plains to Subalpine

Flowering Time:
May to August

Wild Alyssum

Alyssum minus

Mustard Family (Brassicaceae)

Annual, to 10" tall, in dense masses, with rough, hairy stems.

Flowers are very small, stalked, have 4 pale yellow, ⅛" petals, and 4 hairy, grayish sepals. Flowers drop off early. Seed pods are round, compressed, and hairy.

Leaves are spatulate, to 1¼" long, with pointed tips and rough hairs.

Very common in waste areas and fields, along roads and ditches, and on hillsides; European weed.

Life Zones: Plains and Foothills

Flowering Time: March to June

Wintercress

(St. Barbara Weed)

Barbarea orthoceras

Mustard Family (Brassicaceae)

Biennial, to 20" tall, with erect, stout, angular stem.

Flowers are in tight clusters, with 4 yellow, reflexed petals and 4 white and green sepals. Seed pods are linear, to 2" long, angular.

Leaves are soft, fleshy, dark green and purplish; the upper leaves are clasping and the lower leaves are stalked and fiddlelike.

Prefers wet areas, such as irrigated fields, swamps, stream banks, ditches, pastures, and roadsides.

Life Zones: Plains to Montane

Flowering Time: April to September

Buffalo Bur

Solanum rostratum
(Androcera rostrata)

Nightshade Family (Solanaceae)

Annual, to 2' high, with branched, hairy, spiny stems.

Flowers are saucer-shaped, to 1¼" across, on 1" long, spiny, hairy stalks, with yellow corolla and 5 prickly sepals. Fruit is enclosed by the enlarged, spiny calyx.

Leaves are deeply dissected into rounded lobes, with long, hairy, spiny stalks.

Common weed in vacant lots, pastures, roadsides, and fields.

Life Zones:
Plains and Foothills

Flowering Time:
May to September

Ground Cherry

(Virginia Ground Cherry)

Physalis virginiana

Nightshade Family (Solanaceae)

Perennial, bushy, to 2' tall, with stout, hairless, grooved stem.

Flowers are saucer-shaped, nodding, with ¾" stalks. The 5-lobed, pale yellow corolla is lined with purplish pads, and the calyx enlarges into 1" long lobes that enclose the fruit.

Leaves are lance-shaped, to 5" long (including 2" stalks), with wavy to lobed margins.

Common in disturbed soil along roads and streams.

Life Zone: Plains

Flowering Time: June to August

Black Medic

(Yellow Trefoil, Hop Clover)

Medicago lupulina

Pea Family (Fabaceae)

Annual or perennial, to 2' long, with slender, crawling and ascending, grooved, hairy stem, branched at the base.

Flowers are tiny, yellow, in small clusters (to ½" long), with hairy, green and white sepals. Fruit is tiny (³⁄₃₂" across), round, and wrinkled.

Leaves are dissected into 3 oval to round leaflets, toothed around the tip, and hairy on both sides.

Common weed along roads and in gardens, meadows, lawns, and waste places.

Life Zones: Plains and Foothills

Flowering Time: May to October

Golden Banner

(Golden Pea)

Thermopsis divaricarpa
(T. pinetorum)

Pea Family (Fabaceae)

Perennial, to 3' tall, in large patches, with horizontal rootstock and erect, leafy stems.

Flowers to 1" long, in loose clusters, with golden yellow lips and hairy, green, pointed sepals.

Leaves are divided into 3 leaflets and 2 large, leaflike appendages called stipules; both leaflets and stipules are hairy beneath.

Grows abundantly in sandy and gravelly areas of roadsides, valleys, ravines, meadows, and clearings.

Life Zones:
Plains to Subalpine

Flowering Time: April to July

Yellow Sweet Clover

(Honey Clover)

Melilotus officinalis

Pea Family (Fabaceae)

Biennial, to 5' tall, much-branched, with flexible, erect or decumbent stems.

Flowers are pealike, to ¼" long, pale yellow, and fragrant, in tight, 4" long racemes. Seed pods are spine-tipped.

Leaves are divided into 3 leaflets.

Grows in waste places, along roadsides and canals, and near dams and ditches.

Life Zones: Plains to Montane

Flowering Time: June to September

Common Purslane

(Pusley, Verdolagas)

Portulaca oleracea

Purslane Family
(Portulacaceae)

Annual weed with
creeping, much-
branched, fleshy
stem, to 2' long.

Flowers are small (¼"),
with 5 roundish, yellow
to orange petals and
2-parted, keeled calyx.

Leaves are fleshy, spatulate,
to 1" long, shiny, and smooth.

Common in disturbed soil
of fields and pastures, and
along roads and sidewalks;
European immigrant.

Life Zone: Plains

Flowering Time:
June to November

Leafy Spurge

(Leafy Euphorbia, Wolf's Milk)

Tithymalus esula
(Euphorbia esula, E. virgata,
E. intercedans)

Spurge Family
(Euphorbiaceae)

Perennial, to 3'
high, in dense
patches, with milky
juice and much-
branched stems.

Flowers are tiny, greenish yellow,
with yellowish bracts and 4
yellow, crescent-shaped glands.

Leaves are sessile, narrow, to
2½" long, with pointed tips.

Grows in waste places, fields,
and pastures, and along roads;
a noxious weed

Life Zones: Plains to Montane

Flowering Time:
May to September

Rocky Mountain Spurge

(Robust Spurge)

Tithymalus montanus
(T. robustus, T. philcrus,
Euphorbia robusta, E. montana)

Spurge Family (Euphorbiaceae)

Perennial, in patches, to 12" tall, with milky sap and stout, fleshy stem.

Flowers are small, green, and obscured by yellow bracts and 4 crescent-shaped, yellow glands.

Leaves are alternate, to ¾" long, fleshy, and smooth.

Grows on mesas, hillsides, rocky slopes, and other sunny, dry areas; noxious weed.

Life Zones: Plains to Montane

Flowering Time: May to July

Russian Spurge

(Leafy Spurge)

Tithymalus uralensis

Spurge Family (Euphorbiaceae)

Perennial, to 3' tall, in vast colonies, with milky sap and wiry, leafy stems.

Flowers are small and obscured by yellow bracts and crescent-shaped glands.

Leaves are narrow, to ¼" wide, and 2½" long.

Grows along roads and in pastures, fields, and meadows; noxious weed.

Life Zones: Plains to Montane

Flowering Time: June to September

Klamath Weed

(St. John's Weed, St. John's Wort)

Hypericum perforatum

St. Johnswort Family
(Hypericaceae)

Perennial, to 3' tall, in clumps, with tough, smooth stems and opposite branching.

Flowers are starlike, to 1" across, in elongate clusters. The 5 petals are golden yellow and reflexed; the 5 sepals are green and long-tipped; the many stamens are erect, long, and protruding.

Leaves are small, to 1" long, opposite, stalkless, and hairless.

Common along roads, in pastures and fields, and in openings in thickets and woods. *Poisonous.*

Life Zones: Plains to Montane

Flowering Time: June to September

Wood Sorrel

(Yellow Sorrel)

Oxalis stricta

Wood Sorrel Family (Oxalidaceae)

Annual or perennial, to 2" high, with underground runners and a reddish, hairy stem.

Flowers are terminal, with 5 yellow, reflexed petals and hairy, reddish sepals.

Leaves are alternate, divided into 3 leaflets that have a sour taste.

A common nuisance in gardens, lawns, fields, and roadsides; a delicate gem in thickets and woods.

Life Zones: Plains to Montane

Flowering Time: May to October

Candelabra Cactus

(Shrub Cactus, Cane Cactus, Walking Stick,
 Chainlink Cactus, Cholla)

Cylindropuntia imbricata
(Opuntia arborescens, O. imbricata)

Cactus Family (Cactaceae)

Shrub, to 6' tall, with branched,
erect stem made up of 6" long,
spiny pads (joints).

Flowers are large (to 3" wide),
satiny, bright purplish red. Fruit
is yellow, to 1½" long, hairy,
spiny, and edible.

Found in southern Colorado
in deserts and on dry hillsides
and sunny slopes.

Life Zone: Plains

Flowering Time: June and July

New Mexico Locust

Robinia neomexicana

Pea Family (Fabaceae)

Shrub or tree, to 20' tall, with short, reddish brown, hairy branches that bear ½" long spines.

Flowers are in one-sided racemes, with 5 reddish to purplish petals and a bell-shaped, hairy calyx. Pods are sticky, hairy, flat, to 4" long.

Leaves are alternate and pinnately divided into ovate, dark green, hairy leaflets.

Grows on moist sites along streams and roads, in canyons, and on wooded slopes.

Life Zones: Plains and Foothills

Flowering Time: June

Bristle Thistle

(Musk Thistle, Nodding Thistle,
 Pink Thistle)

*Carduus nutans macrolepis
(C. leiophyllus)*

Aster Family (Asteraceae)

Biennial, to 6' tall, with stout, erect to curved stem that has spiny ribs.

Flower heads are large (to 3" wide), often nodding, with no ray flowers; the disk flowers are reddish pink to purplish, and the bracts are stiff, sharp, and broad.

Leaves are alternate, to 16" long, with prickly margins and spiny teeth.

Pest that now grows along roads and in pastures, fields, and ditches; European immigrant.

Life Zones: Plains and Foothills

Flowering Time: June to October

Burdock
(Clotbar)

Arctium minus

Aster Family (Asteraceae)

Biennial, to 6' tall, with erect, grooved, coarse stem.

Flower heads are ½" wide, in clusters, without ray flowers but with many purplish to reddish disk flowers; the bracts are tiered and slender, with hooked tips. Fruit is a nuisance, often clinging to clothing and the hair of animals.

Leaves are large (to 10" by 12"), smooth, and velvety.

Established along roads and fences, in vacant lots, and near streams; European escapee.

Life Zones: Plains and Foothills

Flowering Time: August and September

Indian Blanket

(Firewheel, Gaillardia)
Gaillardia pulchella

Aster Family (Àsteraceae)

Annual, to 32" tall, with grayish, hairy, erect stem.

Flower heads are large (to 2½" across), with red, yellow-tipped ray flowers and purplish red, domed disks.

Leaves are fleshy and stiff, to 3½" long, with bristly, toothed margins.

Grows in open areas and sandy soil, on hillsides and slopes, along roads, and in fields.

Life Zones: Plains and Foothills

Flowering Time: May to July

Ball Nipple Cactus

(Ball Cactus, Nipple Cactus, Cushion Cactus, Pincushion Cactus, Bird's Nest Cactus, Spring Star)

Coryphantha vivipara radiosa
(C. radiosa, Mamillaria vivipara, Cactus vivipara)

Cactus Family (Cactaceae)

Ball-shaped plant, to 3" high, with nipplelike knobs that bear spines; the stout, reddish, central spines are ¾" long, and the lateral spines are ½" long, white, and brown-tipped.

Flowers are spectacular, bright magenta, to 2" across, with fringed petals.

Grows in sandy areas on dry plains and mesas, and in deserts and dry, pine woods in eastern Colorado. This beautiful cactus is threatened.

Life Zones: Plains to Montane

Flowering Time: May to July

Claret Cup Cactus

(Hedgehog Cactus, Pincushion Cactus,
Strawberry Cactus, King's Crown Cactus,
King's Cup Cactus)

Echinocereus triglochidiatus
(E. gonacanthus, E. paucispinus)

Cactus Family (Cactaceae)

Perennial, grows in mounds (to 8"
high) formed from up to 25 round
to cylindric, ribbed, spiny stems.
The spines are clustered (to 12),
stiff, angular, sharp, to 1¼" long.

Flowers are spectacular, brilliant
red, to 3" across, goblet-shaped, with
several petals on a spiny, cobwebby
tube and clumped, yellow and green
stigmas. The fruit is red, plump,
juicy, about 1" long, and edible.

Grows in southern Colorado on dry,
warm hillsides, desert flats, mesas
and ridges, among boulders, and in
open woods. Please help protect this
beauty—it is endangered.

Life Zones: Plains and Foothills

Flowering Time: April and May

246

Hunger Cactus

(Prickly Pear Cactus, Plains Cactus, Starvation Cactus)

Opuntia polyacantha

Cactus Family (Cactaceae)

Perennial, with fleshy, round to oval pads (joints) that are spiny and up to 6" long. Spines are clustered (as many as 9), along with tufts of hair, mostly ½" apart, white to tannish, and to ¾" long.

Flowers are spectacular (to 3" across), with red or yellow, satiny petals. Fruit is fleshy and edible.

Common in dry areas, such as deserts, sunny prairie slopes, and canyon sides.

Life Zones: Plains and Foothills

Flowering Time: May and June

Rocky Mountain Beeplant

(Pink Cleome, Spiderflower, Stinkweed,
Stinking Clover)

Cleome serrulata
(Peritome serrulatum, P. inornatum)

Caper Family (Capparaceae)

Annual, to 5' tall, with erect,
branched stem.

Flowers are in terminal clusters, with
4 pink to purplish or white, ½" long
petals and long, protruding stamens.
Seed pods are pendant, on long stalks,
to 3" long.

Leaves are palmately divided into
3 narrow leaflets.

Grows in sandy soil along roads and
in waste areas, overgrazed pastures,
fallow fields, meadows, and rangeland.

Life Zones: Plains to Montane

Flowering Time: June to August

Scarlet Gaura

(Low Gaura, Butterfly Weed)

Gaura coccinea

Evening Primrose Family (Onagraceae)

Perennial, to 12" tall, in clumps, with leafy, woolly stems.

Flowers are ½" wide, with 4 pink to red petals and a funnel-shaped calyx, with reflexed, woolly lobes. The 8 stamens and long style protrude conspicuously.

Leaves are alternate and crowded, to 1½" long, densely hairy, and grayish green.

Grows in dry areas, such as hillsides, waste places, roadsides, and trailheads.

Life Zones: Plains to Montane

Flowering Time: May to July

Velvetweed

(Lizard Tail, Velvet-Leaved Gaura)

Gaura parviflora

Evening Primrose Family
(Onagraceae)

Biennial, to 7' tall, with erect, much-branched, velvety, sticky stem.

Flowers are tiny, tubular, in long, slender spikes, with 4-lobed, pink corolla and reddish green, reflexed calyx lobes.

Leaves are narrowly lanceolate, to 4" long, velvety, and sticky.

Grows in dry areas of roadsides, ditches, and slopes.

Life Zone: Plains

Flowering Time: July to September

Bunny-in-the-Grass

(Western Figwort, Lanceleaf Figwort)

Scrophularia lanceolata
(S. occidentalis, S. leporella)

Figwort Family (Scrophulariaceae)

Perennial, to 5' tall, with angular, leafy, smooth stem.

Flowers to ½" long, reddish, purplish, and brownish, with erect, 2-lobed upper lip and spreading, 3-lobed lower lip.

Leaves are opposite, to 5" long, with sharp teeth and winged stalks.

Grows in disturbed soil, along roads, fences, and ditches, on rocky hillsides, and in gullies, thickets, and the edges of woods.

Life Zones: Plains to Montane

Flowering Time: May to August

Orange Paintbrush

(Broadbract Paintbrush)

Castilleja integra
(C. gloriosa, C. tomentosa)

Figwort Family (Scrophulariaceae)

Perennial, to 16" high, in clumps, with velvety stems.

Flowers have greenish, inconspicuous corollas, but flashy, red calyx lobes and large, bright red bracts.

Leaves are divided into narrow segments; the lower leaves are entire.

Grows in rocky or gravelly soil along ridges and on hillsides and shrubby slopes. The most common paintbrush of the Plains.

Life Zones: Plains and Foothills

Flowering Time: June to August

Pink Plains Penstemon

(Gilia Penstemon)

Penstemon ambiguus
(Leiostemon ambiguus,
L. purpurea)

Figwort Family
(Scrophulariaceae)

Perennial, to 20" tall, with many woody, slender stems.

Flowers are tubular (to 1⅛" long), narrow, with 5 pink to white corolla lobes that only vaguely resemble the lips of other penstemons.

Leaves are threadlike, opposite, to 1¼" long.

Found on roadsides and sandy hills, and in pastures.

Life Zones: Plains and Foothills

Flowering Time: May to July

Four O'Clock

(Umbrellawort)

Oxybaphus nyctagineus
(Mirabilis nyctaginea, Allonia
nyctaginea, A. floribunda)

Four O'Clock Family
(Nyctaginaceae)

Perennial, to 3' tall, with erect to leaning, grooved, angular stems.

Flowers are in clusters of 3, enclosed by hairy bracts, with 5-lobed, cuplike, pink to magenta or lavender corollas that close during midday.

Leaves are heart-shaped, opposite, to 4" long, dark green on top and pale beneath, with toothed and bristly margins.

Grows in waste places, along roads, and in open woods and fallow fields.

Life Zone: Plains

Flowering Time:
June to October

Hoary Umbrellawort
(Lance-Leaved Wild Four O'Clock)

Oxybaphus hirsutus
(Mirabilis hirsuta, Allionia hirsuta, A. pilosa)

Four O'Clock Family
(Nyctaginaceae)

Perennial, to 3' tall, with erect, flexible, sticky, hairy stem. Blooms at night.

Flowers are in clusters (usually 3 per cluster) that are subtended by bristly, reddish bracts. Flowers have hairy, reddish, petal-like sepals, and no petals.

Leaves are opposite, to 4" long, with blunt tips and long hairs beneath.

Grows in open areas, on sunny slopes and mesas, and along ridges.

Life Zones: Plains and Foothills

Flowering Time:
June to October

Burning Bush

(Ironweed)

Bassia sieversiana
(Kochia sieversiana, K. iranica)

Goosefoot Family (Chenopodiaceae)

Annual, to 5' tall, with erect, branched stem that has a woody base.

Flowers are small, stalkless, in small clusters, with 5 winged sepals.

Leaves are thin, hairy, and often reddish.

Abundant weed along roads, in waste places, on alkali flats, and around ball fields and old dumps; Eurasian immigrant.

Life Zone: Plains

Flowering Time:
July to September

Pinkweed

(Smartweed, Heart's Ease, Pennsylvania Smartweed)

Persicaria pensylvanica
(Polygonum pensylvanicum, P. omissum)

Knotweed Family (Polygonaceae)

Annual, to 30" tall, with slender, jointed, smooth, shiny stems.

Flowers are small (³⁄₁₆"), in spikelike clusters to 1½" long, with pink to purplish, hairy, sticky tepals (undifferentiated petals and sepals).

Leaves are stalked, to 6" long, smooth, and tapered.

Found in wet environments, such as marshes, mud banks, pond and lake shores, and ditches.

Life Zone: Plains

Flowering Time: August and September

Sheep Sorrel

(Common Sorrel, Sour Grass)

Acetosella vulgaris
(Rumex acetosella)

Knotweed Family (Polygonaceae)

Perennial, to 20" tall, with creeping rootstock and erect, slender, ribbed stem.

Flowers are tiny, with whitish petals that turn bright red partway through the season.

Leaves are fleshy, to 3" long, and lobed into arrow-shaped leaflets.

Grows in waste places, disturbed areas, and fields, along roads, and on burned slopes; Eurasian weed.

Life Zones: Plains and Foothills

Flowering Time: May to October

Copper Mallow

(Red Mallow, Scarlet False Mallow,
 Red False Mallow, Cowboy's Delight)

Sphaeralcea coccinea
(Malvastrum coccineum)

Mallow Family (Malvaceae)

Perennial, to 12" tall, with silvery, hairy, leafy stems.

Flowers are saucer-shaped, ¾" across, with 5 orange-red petals.

Leaves are deeply dissected into 3-lobed, rough, silvery segments.

Common in dry areas of fields, roadsides, and shrubby slopes.

Life Zones: Plains and Foothills

Flowering Time: June to September

Wine Cups

(Poppy Mallow, Purple Poppy Mallow)

Callirhoë involucrata

Mallow Family (Malvaceae)

Perennial, with thick taproot and creeping, stout, hairy, twisted stem.

Flowers are stalked and cup-shaped, with 5 satiny, ¾" long, rounded, purplish red petals and 5 green and white, 1" long sepals.

Leaves are on wiry, hairy stalks and are deeply dissected into as many as 7 leathery segments.

Common in waste places and open woods, and on grassy slopes and scrubby hillsides.

Life Zones: Plains and Foothills

Flowering Time: May to August

Butterfly Weed

(Butterfly Milkweed, Orange Milkweed,
 Pleurisy Root, Chigger Flower)

Asclepias tuberosa terminalis

Milkweed Family (Asclepiadaceae)

Perennial, to 3' tall, in clumps,
with thick, tuberous root and
stout, rough, hairy stem.

Flowers are in terminal umbels,
with 5 green sepals hidden by ½"
high, reddish orange petals, with
erect, horned hoods and reflexed
lobes. Fruit is podlike, erect, to
5" long, and smooth.

Leaves are alternate, to 4½" long,
lance-shaped, fuzzy, with undulating
margins.

Grows in dry areas of southern
Colorado, such as roadsides, prairie
slopes, open woods, mesas, and
canyons.

Life Zones: Plains and Foothills

Flowering Time: April to September

Showy Milkweed

(Common Milkweed, Pink
Milkweed, Silkweed, Butterflyweed)

Asclepias speciosa

Milkweed Family (Asclepiadaceae)

Perennial, to 6' tall, with erect,
stout, downy stem.

Flowers are clustered in spherical
umbels (as many as 50 flowers
per umbel), with 5 red, pink, or
purplish petals that are stretched
into hoods (the coronas). Fruit
is duck-shaped, to 4" long, and
covered with knobs and cones.

Leaves are large (to 12" long),
opposite, and soft, with a
prominent, reddish midrib.

Common in sandy and disturbed
areas of fields, roadsides, fence
rows, brushy slopes, and open
woods.

Life Zones: Plains and Foothills

Flowering Time: May to August

Henbit

(Common Henbit, Dead Nettle,
 Common Dead Nettle)

Lamium amplexicaule

Mint Family (Lamiaceae)

Annual, to 8" high, in bunches, with creeping to arching, square stems.

Flowers are tubular, to ¾" long, and 2-lipped; the upper lip is hoodlike and reddish or purplish pink, and the lower lip is notched at the tip and constricted at the base.

Leaves are opposite, to 1½" across, fan-shaped, clasping, and scalloped.

Common in gardens, fields, roadsides, cracks in asphalt, yards, disturbed ground, and waste places; Eurasian import.

Life Zones: Plains and Foothills

Flowering Time: March to October

Woundwort

(Hedgenettle, Betony)

Stachys palustris pilosa

Mint Family (Lamiaceae)

Perennial, to 32" tall, with erect, angular, and hairy stem.

Flowers are ⅝" long, in clusters of 3, each of which is subtended by leaflike bracts; the 3-flowered clusters make up spikes. The corolla is 2-lipped, with the upper lip erect and the lower lip's lobes reflexed and pink to lavender. The calyx is bell-shaped and 5-lobed.

Leaves are opposite, to 3¼" long, toothed, grayish, and hairy beneath.

Grows in moist areas, such as meadows and lake shores, along streams and canals, and in ditches.

Life Zones: Plains to Montane

Flowering Time: June to September

Alsike Clover

Trifolium hybridum

Pea Family (Fabaceae)

Perennial, to 2' high, with erect to arching, hairy stem.

Flowers are in round, dense, 1" clusters, with pink and white corollas.

Leaves are long-stalked, divided into 3 ovate leaflets, hairy beneath.

Common in moist areas along roads and in clearings, meadows, and fields; European immigrant.

Life Zones:
Plains and Foothills

Flowering Time:
June to October

Prairie Clover

(Purple Prairie Clover)

Dalea purpurea
(Petalostemon purpureum)

Pea Family (Fabaceae)

Perennial, to 18" tall, in tufts, with woody root and wiry, yellowish stems.

Flowers are small (³⁄₁₆"), in a tight spike up to 1½" long, with red to purplish petals.

Leaves are palmately divided into 3 to 5, stringlike, 1" long leaflets.

Common in eastern Colorado on prairie slopes, meadows, and shrubby hillsides.

Life Zones: Plains and Foothills

Flowering Time: May to July

Red Clover

Trifolium pratense

Pea Family (Fabaceae)

Perennial, to 30" high, in clumps, with stout, hairy stem.

Flowers are red, pink, purple, and white and crowded into 1½" clusters that are subtended by pairs of leaves.

Leaves are long-stalked and divided into 3 oval leaflets marked by white, V-shaped bands.

Grows in moist areas, such as meadows, pastures, and fields, and along trails and roads.

Life Zones: Plains to Montane

Flowering Time: May to September

Colorado Loco

(Lambert's Loco, Lambert's Red Loco,
Purple Loco)

Oxytropis lambertii

Pea Family (Fabaceae)

Perennial, to 16" tall, in large
patches, with unbranched, leafless,
flower-bearing stalks.

Flowers to 1" long, with bright
purplish-red lips and a sharply
pointed keel.

Leaves are basal, to 12" long,
with several pairs of narrowly
lanceolate leaflets.

Common in dry areas and sandy
soil along roads, in meadows, and
on gravelly slopes. *Very poisonous.*

Life Zones: Plains to Subalpine

Flowering Time: April to August

Crown Vetch
Coronilla varia

Pea Family (Fabaceae)

Perennial, to 4' long, with much-branched, spreading, leaning, angular stems.

Flowers are clustered, umbel-like, with pink to reddish or purplish corollas. Seed pods are slender and erect.

Leaves are divided into paired, short-stalked leaflets (up to 12 pairs, plus a terminal leaflet).

Planted to stabilize highway embankments; escaped to roadsides, ditches, and fields. Eurasian import.

Life Zone: Plains

Flowering Time: June to September

Maiden Pink

Dianthus deltoides

Pink Family (Caryophyllaceae)

Perennial, to 20" tall, with several slender, erect to leaning stems.

Flowers are ½" across, tubular, with pink, magenta, or white petals.

Leaves are narrowly lance-shaped, opposite, and to ¾" long.

Found along roads and on dry slopes; European escapee from cultivation.

Life Zone: Plains

Flowering Time: June to September

Prostrate Vervain

(Bracted Vervain, Large-Bracted Vervain,
Weedy Vervain, Vervain)

Verbena bracteata
(V. bracteosa)

Vervain Family (Verbenaceae)

Perennial, in tufts, creeping, with branched,
hairy stems to 18" long.

Flowers are tiny, arranged in thick,
erect spikes and subtended by 2 stiff,
hairy bracts. Flowers have ³⁄₁₆" long
corolla tube, 5 reflexed, pink to purplish lobes, and a 5-lobed, hairy calyx.

Leaves are 3-lobed, leathery, and hairy, with bristly
margins and fine teeth.

Common on roadsides
and waste ground, and in
ditches, fields, and pastures.

Life Zone: Plains

Flowering Time:
April to October

Showy Vervain

(Wild Verbena, Prairie Verbena, Small-
Flowered Verbena, Dakota Vervain)

Glandularia bipinnatifida
(Verbena bipinnatifida, V. ambrosifolia)

Vervain Family (Verbenaceae)

Perennial, with erect to crawling,
much-branched stems that are up
to 18" long, angular, and bristly.

Flowers are showy, in terminal clusters subtended by long bracts, with
½" long tubular corolla whose 5
pink to lavender lobes are notched.

Leaves are opposite, stalked, and
deeply dissected into 3 segments that
are divided again into pointed lobes.

Abundant in eastern Colorado in
sandy areas, such as roadsides, ditches,
fields, meadows, and rocky slopes.

Life Zones: Plains and Foothills

Flowering Time: April to July

Blue Lettuce

(Blue-Flowered Lettuce, Chicory Lettuce)

Lactuca tataria pulchella

Aster Family (Asteraceae)

Perennial, to 3' tall, with underground rootstock, milky sap, and erect, smooth stem.

Flower heads are in terminal clusters, with no disk flowers, pale blue to lavender ray flowers, and ¾" high sticky, tiered bracts.

Leaves are mostly basal, to 6" long (upper leaves much smaller), with prominent midvein and large teeth.

Found in ditches, fields, meadows, and thickets.

Life Zones: Plains and Foothills

Flowering Time: May to September

Common Chicory

(Blue Sailors, Chicory)

Cichorium intybus

Aster Family (Asteraceae)

Perennial, to 6' tall, with taproot and rigid, branched stem that has milky sap.

Flower heads are large (to 1¾"), with light blue to lavender ray flowers; flowers are open in the morning.

Leaves are mostly basal, to 10" long, deeply incised to merely toothed (stem leaves are much reduced).

Grows along roads and in waste places, fields, and ditches; European import.

Life Zone: Plains

Flowering Time: July to October

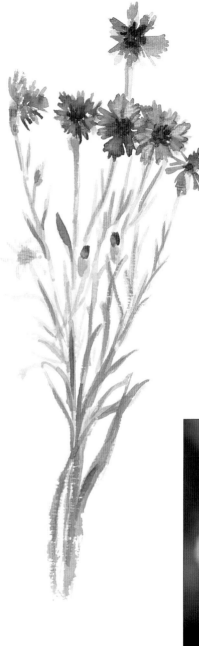

Cornflower

(Bachelor's Button, Knapweed)

Leucacantha cyanus
(Centaurea cyanus)

Aster Family (Asteraceae)

Annual, to 2' tall, in clumps, with erect, leafy stems.

Flower heads are 1½" wide, with bright blue to lavender (or white), funnel-shaped ray flowers and dark red disk flowers.

Leaves are narrow, tapering, and hairy.

Escaped cultivation to waste areas, vacant lots, roadsides, fence rows, and hillsides; European import.

Life Zones: Plains and Foothills

Flowering Time:
July and August

Lanceleaf Chiming Bells

(Narrow-Leaved Mertensia)

Mertensia lanceolata
(M. linearis, M. papillosa)

Borage Family (Boraginaceae)

Perennial, in clumps, to 12" tall, with erect to leaning, flexible stems.

Flowers are small (¾" long), in drooping clusters, with bell-shaped, blue, 5-lobed corolla.

Leaves are bluish green, soft, fleshy, to 3" long, and narrow, with prominent midvein.

Grows in dry places on prairie slopes and shrubby hillsides, and in fields, meadows, and open woods.

Life Zones: Plains to Montane

Flowering Time: May and June

Narrow-Leaved Penstemon

(Light-Blue Beardtongue,
 Skyblue Penstemon)

Penstemon angustifolius

Figwort Family (Scrophulariaceae)

Perennial, to 20" tall, with stout, erect, smooth stem.

Flowers are in raceme, sky blue to pinkish or purplish, with ¾" long, tubular, 2-lipped corolla; the upper lip is 2-lobed, and the lower lip is 3-lobed.

Leaves are fleshy, to 4" long, narrow, with prominent midrib.

Grows in sandy areas, such as vacant lots, fallow fields, and dry hillsides.

Life Zones: Plains and Foothills

Flowering Time: May to July

Blue Flax

(Wild Flax, Prairie Flax, Lewis Flax)

Adenolinum lewisii
(Linum lewisii)

Flax Family (Linaceae)

Perennial, to 3' tall (but blooms when only 2" high), with slender, wiry stems.

Flowers are in open clusters, to 1" across, with 5 pale blue petals, oval sepals, and ball-shaped seed pods.

Leaves are alternate, linear, to 1" long, and grayish green; leaves cover the stem.

Abundant in dry sites, such as roadsides, hillsides, rocky slopes, and forest clearings.

Life Zones: Plains to Subalpine

Flowering Time: May to August

Common Flax

(Cultivated Flax)

Linum usitatissimum

Flax Family (Linaceae)

Annual, to 3' tall, tufted, with smooth, wiry, erect stems.

Flowers are 1" across, with 5 blue to purplish, fan-shaped petals, and 5 pointed sepals with hyaline margins.

Leaves are linear, soft, to 1¼" long.

Grows in waste places, fields, and railroad yards, and along roads; European import.

Life Zone: Plains

Flowering Time: May to September

Prairie Flax

(Meadow Flax, Blue Flax)

Adenolinum pratense
(Linum pratense)

Flax Family (Linaceae)

Annual, to 12" tall, with slender, smooth stems, in clumps; produces flowers when only 3" tall.

Flowers have 5 clawed, pale blue to lavender, ⅜" long petals and 5 ovate sepals with membranous margins.

Leaves are alternate, to ½" long, and narrow; leaves hug the stem.

Grows in exposed areas of prairies, pastures, fields, hillsides, and roadsides.

Life Zone: Plains

Flowering Time: April to June

Geyer Larkspur

(Poison-Weed)

Delphinium geyeri

Hellebore Family (Helleboraceae)

Perennial, to 3' tall, with woody rootstock and erect, grayish, hairy, slender stems.

Flowers are in long, loose clusters, with 5 petal-like, blue to purplish sepals (the uppermost elongated into a spur), and 2 sets of blue petals, with the lower 2 merging into the spur.

Leaves are basal, 5" long, stalked, and dissected into fingerlike, hairy, pointed lobes.

Grows on hillsides, slopes, mesas, and road embankments. *Poisonous* to livestock.

Life Zones: Plains and Foothills

Flowering Time: May to July

Common Skullcap

(Marsh Skullcap, Swamp Skullcap)

Scutellaria galericulata epilobifolia

Mint Family (Lamiaceae)

Perennial, in patches, to 3' tall, with slender, square, leafy, grooved, reddish stems.

Flowers are single, in leaf axils, to ¾" long, pale blue to pinkish or white, and 2-lipped; the upper lip is helmetlike, and the lower lip bends downward.

Leaves are opposite, to 2½" long, lanceolate, and toothed.

Grows on wet sites, such as bogs, meadows, swamps, stream banks, ditches, and lake shores; Eurasian import.

Life Zones: Plains and Foothills

Flowering Time: June to August

Western Spiderwort

(Spiderlily, Spiderwort)

Tradescantia occidentalis
(T. laramiensis, T. universitatis)

Spiderwort Family
(Commelinaceae)

Perennial, to 2' tall, with sticky juice and smooth, jointed stem.

Flowers are large (to 1½" across), in clusters, with 3 blue to purplish, spreading petals and 3 pointed, ½" long sepals. Flowers are open in the morning.

Leaves are long (to 12"), grasslike, and sheathed.

Grows in gravelly areas and on rocky slopes, road embankments, and hillsides.

Life Zones: Plains and Foothills

Flowering Time: June and July

Matrimony Vine

(Wolfberry)

Lycium barbarum
(L. halimifolium)

Nightshade Family (Solanaceae)

Shrub, to 3' high, with arching, leafy stem and slender, tan branches.

Flowers are about ½" across, tubular, in leaf axils, with 5 purple petals that have white streaks, large, protruding anthers, and lobed stigma. Berries are salmon-colored.

Leaves are alternate, slender, to 3" long, short-stalked, thick, and leathery.

Forms thickets around dwellings, along roads, and in ditches.

Life Zones: Plains and Foothills

Flowering Time: June and July

Hoary Aster
(Purple Aster, Pinyon Aster)

Machaeranthera canescens
(M. linearis, M. rubrotinctus,
Aster canescens)

Aster Family (Asteraceae)

Biennial, to 16" tall, with taproot and wiry, grayish, hairy, sticky stem.

Flower heads are clustered, with ⅜" long, purple to bluish ray flowers and sticky, green and white, reflexed bracts in several tiers.

Leaves are narrow, sticky, hairy, and toothed.

Grows in dry places along roads and on slopes and hillsides.

Life Zones:
Plains and Foothills

Flowering Time:
June to October

Violet Aster

(Skyblue Aster)

Aster hesperius
(A. coerulescens, A. fluviatilis)

Aster Family (Asteraceae)

Perennial, to 3' tall, with tough, wiry, reddish, shiny, much-branched stem.

Flower heads to 1" across, in loose clusters, with lavender or pale blue ray flowers, yellow to brownish disks, and 2 tiers of white-margined bracts.

Leaves are tapered at both ends, to 4" long, clasping, smooth, with finely toothed, bristly margins.

Prefers moist areas, such as meadows, pond shores, ditches, canals, and stream banks.

Life Zones: Plains to Montane

Flowering Time: July to September

Gayfeather

(Blazing Star, Dotted Gayfeather)

Liatris punctata
(Lacinaria punctata)

Aster Family (Asteraceae)

Perennial, to 32" tall, with branched, woody rootstock and erect, unbranched stem.

Flower heads are arranged in a narrow spike, have no ray flowers, and only a few (to 8) bright pinkish purple disk flowers with featherlike styles.

Leaves are light green, stiff, to 5" long, ascending, with resin dots.

Common in eastern Colorado in dry, sandy places, such as slopes, roadsides, mesas, and shrubby hillsides.

Life Zones: Plains and Foothills

Flowering Time: July to October

Purple Salsify

(Oyster Plant, Salsify, Goat's Beard)

Tragopogon porrifolius

Aster Family (Asteraceae)

Perennial, to 4' tall, with milky sap and hollow, erect stem.

Flower heads are large (to 4" across), open in morning, without disk flowers but with showy, purple ray flowers (outer ones long, inner ones short), and long, slender bracts. Seed heads are large and round, with silky seeds.

Leaves are grasslike, to 12" long.

Common in waste areas, along roads, canals, and ditches, and in fields.

Life Zones: Plains and Foothills

Flowering Time: June to August

Skeleton Plant

(Skeleton Weed, Rush Pink, Milk Pink)

Lygodesmia juncea

Aster Family (Asteraceae)

Perennial, to 18" tall, with deep rootstock and erect, rigid, smooth, much-branched stem.

Flower heads are not asterlike, with no disk flowers and only 5 broad, purple, petal-like ray flowers; however, the ½" high whorl of several rows of slender bracts definitely fits the aster family.

Leaves are rigid, triangular, inconspicuous, less than ¼" long.

Grows in dry areas, disturbed soil, on gravelly slopes, and along roads.

Life Zone: Plains

Flowering Time: June to August

Bull Thistle

(Common Thistle, Bur Thistle)

Cirsium vulgare
(C. lanceolatum, Carduus lanceolatus)

Aster Family (Asteraceae)

Biennial, to 6' tall, with a low, basal rosette the first year and erect, leafy stems the second year.

Flower heads are large (to 2½" high), without disk flowers; the ray flowers are purple, and the bracts have sharp spines.

Leaves are lanceolate, extending down the stem, with spiny teeth.

Common along roads, in waste places, ditches, pastures, and fields, and on hillsides; Eurasian immigrant.

Life Zones: Plains and Foothills

Flowering Time: July to September

Canada Thistle

(Creeping Thistle)

Cirsium arvense
(Carduus arvensis)

Aster Family (Asteraceae)

Perennial, to 6' tall, in dense patches, with creeping rootstock and much-branched stems.

Flower heads are many, ¾" high, without ray flowers; disk flowers are purple to pinkish, or white.

Leaves are coarse-toothed, to 4" long, with ⅛" long spines.

A pest in towns, ball fields, gardens and fields, pastures and waste places; Eurasian immigrant.

Life Zone: Plains

Flowering Time: July to September

Bellflower

(Harebell, Grandmother's Bluebell)
Campanula rapunculoides
Bellflower Family (Campanulaceae)

Perennial, to 2½' tall, in clumps, with deep rootstock and angular, twisted, purplish stem.

Flowers are in one-sided racemes, with pale purple, 1¼" high corolla.

Leaves are stalked, to 3" long, rough, with toothed margins; the upper leaves are much smaller than the lower leaves.

Found in abandoned gardens and yards, and along roads and ditches; European escapee from cultivation.

Life Zones: Plains and Foothills

Flowering Time: June to October

Pasque Flower

(American Pasqueflower, Wild Crocus, Prairie Anemone, Lion's Head, Blue Tulip, Windflower)

Pulsatilla patens hirsutissima
(P. hirsutissima, P. ludoviciana, Anemone patens)

Buttercup Family (Ranunculaceae)

Perennial, to 15" tall, with thick taproot and hollow flower stalk.

Flowers to 2" across, single, without petals, but with 5 to 7 petal-like sepals that are lavender to purple, hairy outside, and paler inside. Seeds have 1" long, hairy plumes.

Leaves are basal and divided into narrow, sharply pointed segments.

Grows on hillsides and slopes, and in meadows, fields, open woods, forest clearings, sagebrush, and even tundra.

Life Zones: Plains to Alpine

Flowerng Time: March to August

Periwinkle

(Myrtle)

Vinca minor

Dogbane Family (Apocynaceae)

Perennial, to 8" high, in dense patches, with flexible, yellowish stems to 3' long.

Flower is single, 1" across, with 5 reflexed, bluish purple petals.

Leaves are opposite, evergreen, leathery, to 1½" long, shiny on top and pale beneath.

Found in shaded areas and open woods, around abandoned houses, and along roads; Eurasian escapee from cultivation.

Life Zones: Plains and Foothills

Flowering Time:
February to November

Sticky Willowherb

(Northern Willowherb)

Epilobium ciliatum
(E. adenocaulon, E. glandulosum,
E. brevistylum)

Evening Primrose Family
(Onagraceae)

Perennial, to 3' high, with fleshy bulbs and angular, sticky stems.

Flowers to 1" across, tubular, with lavender, blue, or pink petals and slender, 2½", bean-like pods.

Leaves are thick, elliptical to lanceolate, to 2½" long, with small teeth.

Common near moist areas, such as swamps, springs, thickets, streams, and ditches.

Life Zones: Plains to Montane

Flowering Time:
June to September

Orchid Beardtongue

(One-Sided Penstemon, Sidebells Penstemon, Purple Beardtongue)

Penstemon secundiflorus

Figwort Family (Scrophulariaceae)

Perennial, to 20" tall, with unbranched, erect, smooth stem.

Flowers are in one-sided raceme, about 1" long, magenta to lavender, with 2-lobed upper lip and 3-lobed lower lip.

Leaves are opposite, ovate, to 4" long, fleshy, soft, pale bluish green, and clasping.

Common in dry and sandy areas, such as hillsides, roadsides, slopes, fields, and pastures.

Life Zones: Plains to Montane

Flowering Time: May to July

American Speedwell

(American Brooklime,
 Water Speedwell)

Veronica americana

Figwort Family
(Scrophulariaceae)

Perennial, to 30" high, with trailing to erect, slender, smooth stem.

Flowers are ¼" across, clustered in leaf axils, with 4 round, bluish purple petals.

Leaves are opposite, to 3" long, clasping; the lower leaves are short-stalked.

Common in wet environments, such as marshes, stream banks, ditches, and springs; may even grow in shallow water.

Life Zones: Plains and Foothills

Flowering Time: May to August

Chain Speedwell

Veronica catenata
(V. salina, V. connata)

Figwort Family
(Scrophulariaceae)

Perennial, to 16" tall, with erect or bent, grayish stem.

Flowers are small (about 3/16" across), in axillary racemes, with 4 lavender, pinkish, bluish, or whitish petals.

Leaves are opposite, clasping, to 3" long, narrowly lance-shaped, smooth, with short teeth.

Common in mud along streams; sometimes grows in water.

Life Zones: Plains and Foothills

Flowering Time: May and June

Tulip Gentian

(Prairie Gentian, Bluebell,
 Lira de San Pedro)

Eustoma grandiflorum
(E. russellianum, E. andrewsii)

Gentian Family (Gentianaceae)

Perennial, to 2' tall, with taproot
and erect, bluish green stem.

Flowers are showy and large
(to 1½" across), bell-shaped,
with 5 sharp sepals and 5 oval,
purple and pinkish petals.

Leaves are opposite, clasping,
bluish green, to 2" long, with
3 prominent veins.

Grows in eastern Colorado in grassy
areas, moist meadows, and fields,
and on flood plains. This beautiful
gentian is almost extinct. The
photograph shows a dried specimen,
courtesy of the Kathryn Kalmbach
Herbarium, Denver Botanic Gardens.

Life Zone: Plains

Flowering Time: June to September

Storksbill

(Filaree, Cranesbill, Alfileria, Redstem,
 Heronbill, Pinclover)

Erodium cicutarium

Geranium Family (Geraniaceae)

Annual that overwinters, to
3" high, with red, creeping, much-
branched stem.

Flowers are ½" across, in clusters
on hairy stalks, with 5 lavender,
pinkish, or white petals. Fruit
is long, slender, and resembles
a stork's bill.

Leaves are long-stalked and
pinnately dissected into grayish
green, toothed lobes.

Abundant in sandy areas along
roads, in yards, fallow fields,
and overgrazed pastures, and
in asphalt fissures and concrete
cracks; European immigrant.

Life Zones: Plains and Foothills

Flowering Time:
February to November

Early Larkspur

(Low Larkspur, Nelson's Larkspur)

Delphinium nuttallianum
(D. nelsonii)

Hellebore Family (Helleboraceae)

Perennial, to 12" tall, in large patches, with slender, smooth stem.

Flowers are in open clusters, with 5 purple, petal-like sepals, one of which is spurred, and 4 purple, ¾" long petals.

Leaves are long-stalked and deeply dissected into fingerlike lobes.

Grows in meadows, fields, thickets, and woods. *Caution:* its tuberlike roots are poisonous.

Life Zones: Plains to Montane

Flowering Time: May and June

Grape Hyacinth

Muscari botryoides

Lily Family (Liliaceae)

Perennial, to 10" tall, with bulb and several fleshy, erect flower stems.

Flowers are stalked, ¼" long, purple, dark blue, or sometimes white, in a dense raceme.

Leaves (2 per plant) are grasslike, to 10" long, flat, thick, and basal.

Grows along fences, roads, fields, and pastures; escapee from cultivation.

Life Zone: Plains

Flowering Time: March to May

Purple Loosestrife

Lythrum salicaria

Loosestrife Family (Lythraceae)

Perennial, to 5' tall, with stout, erect, angular, smooth stem.

Flowers are ½" across, in paired clusters on long spikes, with 6 reddish purple petals, bristly calyx, and 12 purple, protruding stamens.

Leaves are opposite, to 4" long, broadly lance-shaped, pointed, and clasping.

Grows in ditches and swamps, and along shores. This European pest is destroying wetlands and needs to be eradicated. Report its presence to the Colorado Division of Wildlife.

Life Zone: Plains

Flowering Time: July to September

American Germander

(Germander, Woodsage)

Teucrium canadense occidentale

Mint Family (Lamiaceae)

Perennial, to 26" tall, with creeping rootstock and erect, angular, hairy stem.

Flowers are pinkish purple, in compact spikes, 2-lipped, with the upper lip split into 2 erect lobes; the calyx is sticky and hairy.

Leaves are opposite, to 4" long, hairy beneath, and toothed.

Grows in wet places, such as ditches, swamps, pond shores, stream banks, meadows, and woods.

Life Zones: Plains and Foothills

Flowering Time: June to August

Horsemint

(Pink Pergamot, Wild Pergamot,
 Beebalm, Mintleaf Beebalm,
 Lemon Mint)

Monarda fistulosa menthifolia

Mint Family (Lamiaceae)

Perennial, to 3' tall, in clumps, with erect, unbranched, square stem.

Flowers are in crowded, roundish clusters, 3" across, with purple and pink, 2-lipped petals, and a hairy, spiny calyx.

Leaves are opposite, 3½" long, bright green, with toothed margins and mint odor.

Common on sunny hillsides and slopes, and in gullies and open woods.

Life Zones: Plains to Montane

Flowering Time: June to August

Wild Mint

(Field Mint)

Mentha arvensis
(M. penardi, M. glabrior,
M. borealis, M. canadensis)

Mint Family (Lamiaceae)

Perennial, to 3' tall, aromatic, in patches, with creeping rootstock and erect, square, slender, purplish stem.

Flowers are small (to ¼"), clustered in leaf axils, pinkish purple, and 2-lipped; the upper lip is notched, and the lower one is 3-lobed.

Leaves are opposite, to 3" long, with pointed tip and short, sharp teeth.

Thrives in moist sites, such as shores, stream banks, bogs, irrigation ditches, and wet woods.

Life Zones: Plains and Foothills

Flowering Time: June to October

Bush Morning Glory

(Morning Glory,
Old-Man-of-the-Earth)

Ipomoea leptophylla

Morning Glory Family (Convolvulaceae)

Perennial, to 4' high, bushy, with robust, smooth, flexible, much-branched stems. Plant has enormous roots that can be as thick as fence posts, weigh as much as 25 pounds, and live up to 50 years or more.

Flowers are large (2½" wide), funnel-shaped, and pinkish purple.

Leaves are narrow, to 4" long, with short stalks.

Grows in dry areas in disturbed soil, along roads, and on prairie slopes.

Life Zone: Plains

Flowering Time: June to August

Purple Mustard
(Blue Mustard, Spring Purple Weed)
Chorispora tenella
Mustard Family (Brassicaceae)

Annual, to 20" high, in large patches, with stout, fleshy stem.

Flowers are tubular, in open racemes, with 4 purple to pinkish, spatulate petals.

Leaves are mostly basal, fleshy, with wavy to toothed margins.

Common Asian import; grows along roads and in vacant lots and fallow fields.

Life Zone: Plains

Flowering Time: April to June

Alfalfa
(Medick, Medic, Lucerne)
Medicago sativa

Pea Family (Fabaceae)

Perennial, to 3' tall, with taproot and slender, flexible, leaning stem.

Flowers are small, in elongate clusters (to 2" long), with purple, 2-lipped, ⅜" long corolla. Seed pods are coiled or sickle-shaped.

Leaves are divided into leaflets that are 1" long and toothed.

Found in gardens, lawns, fallow fields and along roads; escapee from cultivation.

Life Zone: Plains

Flowering Time: May to October

Field Milkvetch

(Purple Milkvetch, Fragrant Violet Milkvetch)

Astragalus agrestis
(A. dasyglottis, A. hypoglottis, A. virgultulus,
A. bracteatus, A. goniatus)

Pea Family (Fabaceae)

Perennial, in clumps, with 12" long, slender, hairy, leaning stems.

Flowers are in crowded, roundish clusters, with purple, ¾" long corolla and black-haired calyx.

Leaves are pinnately dissected into as many as 21 leaflets, ¾" long.

Grows in moist, cool environments, such as grassy meadows, gullies, streams, ditches, and brushy slopes.

Life Zones: Plains to Montane

Flowering Time: May to August

Purple Peavine

(Purple Vetch, Wild Sweet Pea)

Lathyrus eucosmus
(L. decaphyllus)

Pea Family (Fabaceae)

Perennial vine, climbing or trailing, with angular stems to 20" long.

Flowers are in racemes, with 1" long, purple banner, pinkish wings, and whitish keel.

Leaves are pinnately divided into thick, smooth, 2½" long leaflets and have a terminal bristle or clasping tendril.

Grows in exposed areas, such as hillsides and slopes, gulches, and open thickets and woods.

Life Zones: Plains to Montane

Flowering Time: May to July

American Vetch

(Wild Pea, Blue Vetch)

Vicia americana

Pea Family (Fabaceae)

Perennial vine, prostrate or climbing via tendrils, with slender, square, smooth stems, to 4' in length.

Flowers are in loose racemes, with 1¼", 2-lipped, purple or reddish corolla. Seed pod is flat, 2" long.

Leaves are pinnately compound, with 1¾" leaflets and a clasping tendril at the tip.

Grows in meadows, on grassy slopes and hillsides, in thickets and openings in woods, and along roadsides and fences.

Life Zones: Plains to Montane

Flowering Time: May to August

Early Purple Vetch

(Leatherpod Loco)

Astragalus shortianus
(Xylophacys shortianus)

Pea Family (Fabiaceae)

Perennial, to 6" high, with stout, wiry, leaning flower stems.

Flowers in short, crowded cluster, purple to pinkish, with slender, hairy calyx lobes. Seed pods are hairy, 1¼" long, and become leathery.

Leaves are pinnately divided into paired leaflets—to 10, plus a terminal one—that are hairy, grayish, oval, and ½" long.

Found on dry slopes and hillsides, along roads and embankments.

Life Zones: Plains and Foothills

Flowering Time: April to June

Tiny Trumpet

(Collomia)

Collomia linearis

Phlox Family (Polemoniaceae)

Annual, to 10" high, with slender, unbranched, leafy, reddish stem.

Flowers are trumpet-shaped, ½" long, with lavender or pinkish 5-lobed corolla and 5-lobed, cup-shaped, bristly calyx.

Leaves are alternate, fleshy, narrow, and pointed, and hug the stem.

Common in sagebrush and on scrub oak hillsides, in prairies, and near roads and other disturbed areas.

Life Zones: Plains to Montane

Flowering Time: May to August

Blue Vervain

Verbena hastata

Vervain Family (Verbenaceae)

Annual, to 3' tall, with erect, hollow, angular, purplish stem.

Flowers are small, with purple to bluish, 5-lobed, ⅜" wide corolla, in erect, slender spikes that form a tight panicle.

Leaves are opposite, short-stalked, to 6" long, bristly beneath, with toothed margins.

Grows in wet places, such as ditches, marshes, stream banks, and pond shores.

Life Zones: Plains to Foothills

Flowering Time: July to September

Glossary

I have substituted English for "botanese" wherever possible in this book. However, some botanical terms cannot be avoided—there simply are no English substitutes—and certain English terms have specific meanings in botany and, therefore, need to be defined. The following illustrations show typical and/or common flower and leaf types. For written descriptions, and for definitions of other terms used in this guide, see the list of terms that follows the illustrations.

SIMPLE FLOWER

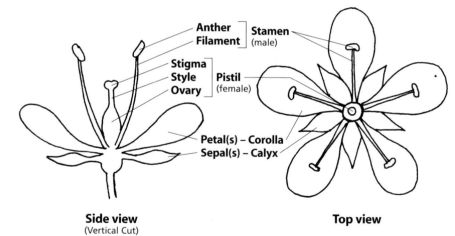

Anther ⎤ Stamen
Filament ⎦ (male)

Stigma ⎤
Style ⎥ Pistil
Ovary ⎦ (female)

Petal(s) – Corolla
Sepal(s) – Calyx

Side view
(Vertical Cut)

Top view

COMPOSITE FLOWER HEAD

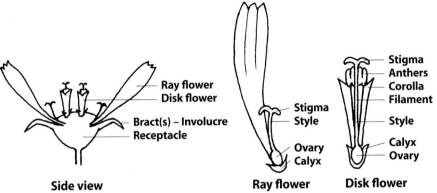

Ray flower
Disk flower

Bract(s) – Involucre
Receptacle

Stigma
Style

Ovary
Calyx

Stigma
Anthers
Corolla
Filament

Style

Calyx
Ovary

Side view
(Vertical Cut)

Ray flower

Disk flower

PEA FLOWER

GRASS SPIKELET

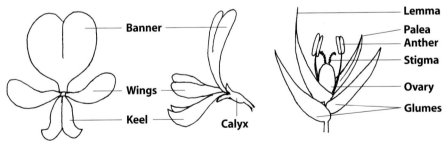

Banner

Wings

Keel

Calyx

Front View

Side View

Lemma
Palea
Anther
Stigma

Ovary

Glumes

INFLORESCENCES

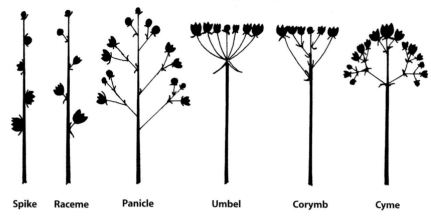

| Spike | Raceme | Panicle | Umbel | Corymb | Cyme |

SIMPLE LEAVES

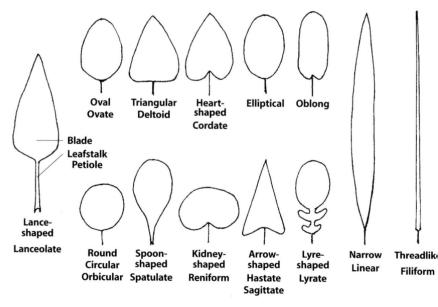

Oval
Ovate

Triangular
Deltoid

Heart-
shaped
Cordate

Elliptical

Oblong

Blade
Leafstalk
Petiole

Lance-
shaped
Lanceolate

Round
Circular
Orbicular

Spoon-
shaped
Spatulate

Kidney-
shaped
Reniform

Arrow-
shaped
Hastate
Sagittate

Lyre-
shaped
Lyrate

Narrow
Linear

Threadlike
Filiform

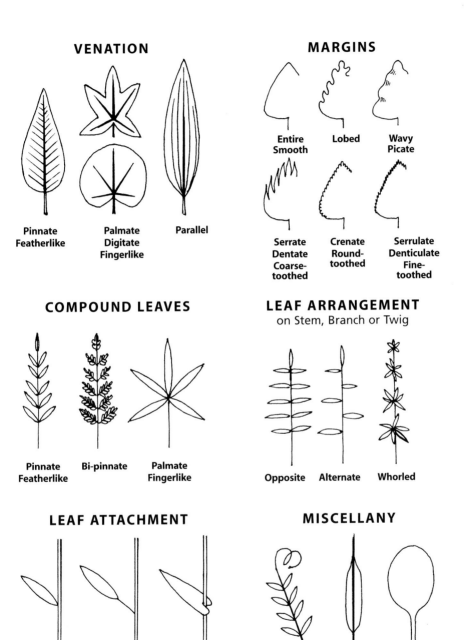

VENATION

Pinnate
Featherlike

Palmate
Digitate
Fingerlike

Parallel

MARGINS

Entire
Smooth

Lobed

Wavy
Picate

Serrate
Dentate
Coarse-
toothed

Crenate
Round-
toothed

Serrulate
Denticulate
Fine-
toothed

COMPOUND LEAVES

Pinnate
Featherlike

Bi-pinnate

Palmate
Fingerlike

LEAF ARRANGEMENT
on Stem, Branch or Twig

Opposite

Alternate

Whorled

LEAF ATTACHMENT

Sessile
Stalkless

Stalked
Petioled
Petiolate

Clasping

MISCELLANY

Tendril

Winged
Stalk

Clawed
Petal

Alternate One branch or leaf per node.

Annual A plant that lives one year.

Anther The flower organ that produces pollen.

Ascending Growing upward at an angle.

Awn A slender bristle or spine; used to describe grasses.

Axil The angle formed by a stem and its leaf.

Banner Upper, upright petal of a pea-type flower; also called the standard.

Biennial A plant that lives two years.

Bract A modified leaf below a flower or inflorescence.

Calyx Collective term for the sepals of a flower.

Claw Narrow stalk of petal.

Cleft Deeply cut.

Corm Thickened, vertical, underground stem.

Corolla Collective term for the petals of a flower.

Culm Stem of grasses, sedges, and rushes.

Decumbent Bent at the base, prostrate; usually used to describe stems.

Deltoid Triangular.

Entire Continuous margin of leaf, i.e., without lobes or teeth.

Fascicle Bundle of needles, spines, or bristles.

Filament Stalk supporting anthers.

Floret Small flower; used to describe grasses.

Glumes The two outer husks or bracts of a grass spikelet.

Hyaline Translucent, membranous.

Inflated Expanded, bulging, bloated.

Inflorescence Collective term for the flowers on a stem; cluster of flowers.

Involucre Ring of leaflike bracts below a flower cluster.

Keel Ridge or spine; the fused lower petals of a pea-type flower.

Krummholz Bent, stunted tree (usually at timberline)

Lanceolate Shaped like the head of a lance or spear.

Lemma Outer bract of a grass flower.

Lenticel Horizontal slit in bark.

Linear Narrow and long, with parallel margins.

Nerve Vein of leaf (or of other plant part)

Node The point on a stem where branches or leaves arise.

Opposite Branching in pairs.

Ovate Oval, egg-shaped.

Palea Inner bract of a grass flower.

Palmate Spreading like the fingers of a hand.

Panicle A much-branched inflorescence of stalked flowers.

Pedicel Flower stalk.

Peduncle Stalk of a flower cluster.

Perennial Plant that lives three years or longer.

Petiole Leaf stalk.

Pinnate Featherlike.

Pistil The seed-producing organ of a flower.

Raceme An inflorescence with stalked flowers along a stem.

Ray flower The outer flower of a composite flower head (used with Aster Family).

Reflexed Bent abruptly backward.

Rhizome Underground stem; rootstock.

Rootstock Underground stem; rhizome.

Rosette Ring or cluster of bracts or leaves; basal leaf cluster.

Scale Thin, transparent bract; used to describe sedges.

Sessile Without a stalk.

Spatulate Shaped like a spatula or spoon; narrowing toward the base.

Spike Inflorescence with stalkless flowers along a stem.

Spikelet Small flower cluster of grasses and sedges.

Stamen Male organ of a flower; consists of the filament and anthers.

Stigma The tip of the pistil where pollen is trapped.

Stipule Small, leaflike appendage at the base of a leaf.

Stolon A horizontal shoot that puts down roots; runner.

Style Stalklike part of the pistil.

Subtending Closely underlying or attached below; often used to describe bracts under a flower cluster.

Tendril Slender, clasping appendage (modified leaf or leaflet) that attaches a plant to something else.

Tepals Sepals and petals that are indistinguishable from each other.

Tuft Tight cluster of stems, bristles, or hairs; used to describe grasses and sedges.

Umbel Flower cluster whose stalks radiate from a common center.

Whorl Three or more leaves at one node.

Wing A thin, flat extension. Examples: winged stalk, winged fruit, winged seed. Also, one of the lateral petals of a pea-type flower.

Index of Common Names

Index of Latin Names

Index of Plant Families

Selected References

Baerg, Harry J. *How to Know the Western Trees*, 2nd edition. Dubuque, Iowa: William C. Brown Company Publishers, 1973.

Beaudoin, Viola Kneeland. *The Beaudoin Easy Method of Identifying Wildflowers*. Aurora, Colorado: Evergreen Publishing Company, 1983.

Clements, Frederic F. and Clements, Edith S. *Rocky Mountain Flowers*. New York: Hafner Publishing Company, 1963.

Craighead, John J.; Craighead, Frank C. Jr.; and Davis, Ray J. *A Field Guide to Rocky Mountain Wildflowers*. Peterson Field Guide Series. Boston: Houghton Mifflin Company, 1963.

Cronquist, Arthur, et al. *Intermountain Flora, Vascular Plants of the Intermountain West*, Volumes 1-6. Bronx, New York: New York Botanical Garden, 1972-1994.

Duft, Joseph F. and Moseley, Robert K. *Alpine Wildflowers of the Rocky Mountains*. Missoula, Montana: Mountain Press Publishing, 1989.

Elias, Thomas S. *Trees of North America*. Outdoor Life/Nature Books. New York: Van Nostrand Reinhold Company, 1980.

Forey, Pamela. *Wild Flowers*. American Nature Guides. New York: Gallery Books, W. H. Smith Publishers, Inc., 1990.

Gould, Frank W. *Grasses of the Southwestern United States*. Tucson, Arizona: University of Arizona Press, 1973.

Harrington, H. D. *Manual of the Plants of Colorado*. Denver: Sage Books, 1954.

Hermann, Frederick J. *Manual of the Carices of the Rocky Mountains and Colorado Basin*. Agriculture Handbook No. 374. Washington, D.C.: U.S. Dept. Agriculture, 1970.

Kelly, George W. *A Guide to the Woody Plants of Colorado*. Boulder, Colorado: Pruett Publishing Company, 1970.

Kirkpatrick, Zoe Merriman. *Wildflowers of the Western Plains: A Field Guide*. Austin, Texas: University of Texas Press, 1992.

Nelson, Ruth Ashton, and Williams, Roger L. *Handbook of Rocky Mountain Plants*. Niwot, Colorado: Roberts Rinehart Publishers, 1992.

Orr, Robert T. and Orr, Margaret C. *Wildflowers of Western America*. New York: Alfred A. Knopf, Inc., 1974.

Pesman, M. Walter. *Meet the Natives*. 9th edition. Colorado: Denver Botanic Gardens & Roberts Rinehart Publishers, 1992.

Pohl, Richard W. *How to Know the Grasses*. Dubuque, Iowa: William C. Brown Company Publishers, 1953.

Porsild, A. E. *Rocky Mountain Wild Flowers*. Ottawa, Canada: National Museum of Canada, 1979.

Reynolds, William. *Wildflowers of America*. New York: Gallery Books, W. H. Smith Publishers Inc., 1987.

Rickett, Harold William. *Wild Flowers of the United States*, Volume 6, New York: McGraw-Hill Book Company, 1973.

Spellenberg, Richard. *The Audubon Society Field Guide to North American Wildflowers, Western Region*. New York: Alfred A. Knopf, 1987.

Strickler, Dee. *Prairie Wildflowers*. Columbia Falls, Montana: Flower Press, 1986.

———. *Forest Wildflowers*. Columbia Falls, Montana: Flower Press, 1988.

———. *Alpine Wildflowers*. Columbia Falls, Montana: Flower Press, 1990.

Venning, Frank D. and Saito, Manahu C. *A Guide to Field Identification, Wildflowers of North America*. New York: Golden Press, 1984.

Walcott, Mary Vaux; Platt, Dorothy Falcon; and Rickett, H. W. *Wildflowers of America*. New York: Crown Publishers, Inc., 1969.

Weber, William A. *Colorado Flora, Western Slope*. Boulder, Colorado: Associated University Press, 1987.

———. *Colorado Flora, Eastern Slope*. Niwot, Colorado: University Press of Colorado, 1990.

Willard, Bettie E., and Smithson, Michael T. *Alpine Wildflowers of the Rocky Mountains*. Estes Park, Colorado: Rocky Mountain Nature Association, 1988.

Williams, Jean, et al. *Rocky Mountain Alpines*. Portland, Oregon: Timber Press, 1986.

Wingate, Janet L. *A Simplified Guide to Common Colorado Grasses*. Privately published, 1986.

———. *Rocky Mountain Flower Finder*. Berkeley, California: Nature Study Guild, 1990.

Young, Robert G. and Young, Joann W. *Colorado West, Land of Geology and Wildflowers*. Salt Lake City, Utah: Artistic Printing Company, 1984.

Zwinger, Ann H. and Willard, Beatrice F. *Land Above the Trees*. New York: Harper and Row, Publishers, 1972.

ABOUT THE AUTHOR

PHOTO BY: BILL BURGER

Dr. G. K. "Joe" Guennel has lived in Colorado for almost 35 years and has made a name for himself in science and sports.

Born in Germany, Joe grew up in Pennsylvania and later moved to Indiana, where he attended Butler University in Indianapolis. During World War II, he served in the United States Army, with the infantry in 1944 and 1945 in France, Germany, and Austria. After the war, he worked for the U.S. military government as a civilian in Karlsruhe, West Germany, where he married Hilde E. Lang in 1947. He returned to Butler University to earn an M.S. degree in botany and later received a Ph.D. in botany from Indiana University.

For twelve years Joe worked for the Indiana Geological Survey, conducting research in palynology (the study of spores and pollen) and earning a worldwide reputation. He has been recognized in *American Men and Women of Science, Who's Who in the West,* and the international publication, *Men of Achievement.*

In 1961 Joe and Hilde moved to Colorado, where Joe joined Marathon Oil Company's Research Center in Littleton. Active in community sports as a coach and organizer, he is known as "the father of Colorado soccer" and is a member of the Colorado Sports Hall of Fame. He has been inducted into the National Soccer Hall of Fame in Oneanta, New York, for his work promoting soccer in the Midwest and Rocky Mountain region.

After retiring, Joe undertook an intensive study of the flora of Colorado, painting, photographing, and describing plants throughout the state, as well as cataloging slides and specimens he collected over the years while hiking and climbing. He has compiled and organized his work into this two-volume set, *Guide to Colorado Wildflowers.*